DEAD FAMOUS

SPARTACUS
AND HIS GLORIOUS GLADIATORS

by Toby Brown

Illustrated by Clive Goddard

Hippo

For Farne, who had to live with me and
Spartacus in a small flat for two years

Scholastic Children's Books,
Euston House, 21 Eversholt Street,
London NW1 1DB, UK

A division of Scholastic Ltd
London ~ New York ~ Toronto ~ Sydney ~ Auckland
Mexico City ~ New Delhi ~ Hong Kong

Published in the UK by Scholastic Ltd, 2004

Text copyright © Toby Brown, 2004
Illustrations copyright © Clive Goddard, 2004

10 digit ISBN 0 439 98187 5
13 digit ISBN 978 0439 98187 3

Typeset by M Rules
Printed in the UK by CPI Bookmarque, Croydon, CR0 4TD

14 16 18 20 19 17 15 13

The rights of Toby Brown and Clive Goddard to be identified as the
author and illustrator respectively of this work has been asserted by them
in accordance with the Copyright, Designs and Patents Act, 1988.

Papers used by Scholastic Children's Books are made from wood
grown in sustainable forests.

Introduction   5

From shepherd to soldier to slave   8

Glorious gladiators and bloody arenas   27

The big breakfast breakout   44

The gladi-crater   53

The three thugs   70

No gold, just iron   85

Two consuls, four legions and   99
a funeral

Rome or home?   112

Lethal lotteries and marine monsters   124

The wall of death   140

'I'm Spartacus!'   152

Epilogue   173

INTRODUCTION

He wasn't rich, he wasn't a king, an emperor or an inventor or anything like that. In fact Spartacus was just a slave. So why is it that 2,000 years after he lived his name has inspired films, books and revolutions all over the world? Just why exactly is he dead famous?

HE WAS A GREAT GLADIATOR!

HE FOUGHT THE ROMANS!

OK, so he did some pretty spectacular things. But the fact is that he didn't just fight the Romans. Spartacus, along with his army of freed slaves, actually BEAT them. For the Romans, having a bunch of scruffy slaves defeat their crack troops in battle was really embarrassing. But it was even worse that a gladiator led the slave army. To them, gladiators were the lowest of the low.

Roman historians preferred to write about 'Great Men'. Plenty was written about Roman emperors and generals but the writers played down the more awkward episodes in their history. Only a few wrote about Spartacus and his slave army ... they were probably just a bit embarrassed about it all.

One of the historians who *did* write about Spartacus was a man called Sallust. He was in his teens when Spartacus was fighting in the arena. Fortunately for us Sallust wrote a detailed account of the slave war against the Romans. Unfortunately for us only fragments of his history survived.

Fortunately for us, a few years later other Roman writers also recorded the story. Unfortunately for us these later historians often don't agree with one another. But this book pieces together the history of Spartacus's amazing life. Where the Roman writers don't agree, or have left things out, this book will tell you what *probably* happened.

Sallust described Spartacus as having 'immense bodily strength and spirit' – being a gladiator *and* the leader of an army definitely required both of these. But Sallust never described his face. In fact no one even knew what Spartacus looked like until 1960. That's when a film about him came out starring an actor called Kirk Douglas. Ask any adult what Spartacus looked like and they'll say he had spiky blonde hair, piercing blue eyes and a chin with a dimple right in the middle. Of course, the Hollywood version didn't show that he probably had dark hair, a broken nose and several missing teeth. That's the problem with Hollywood: they try to clean up history so it looks good on film.

But this book isn't going to clean up anything. So if you don't like stories of battles and bloodshed, gladiators and gore, stop reading now. You do? Well read on and find out how a shepherd boy from Thrace suffered the hardships of life as a Roman soldier, went on to face death every day as a gladiator, marched the length of Italy (twice) *and* led a huge army against the fearsome Roman legions. Read Spartacus's diary to find out how he shook the mighty city of Rome and keep abreast of the latest battle action in *The Legion* newspaper.

Get ready for the adventure story of a lifetime...

FROM SHEPHERD TO SOLDIER TO SLAVE

THE ROMAN REPUBLIC

BRITAIN

GAUL

GERMANIA

WESTERN THRACE - BIRTHPLACE OF SPARTACUS

ITALY

ROME

CARTHAGE

BYTHINIA AND PONTUS

Spartacus was born around 100 BC in a place called Thrace (now called Bulgaria).

Apart from a few mountain areas in the middle, Thrace was covered in trees. The people of Thrace were divided into dozens of different tribes, all with their own territory amongst the forests and on the mountainsides.

Spartacus and his family belonged to a tribe called the Maidoi. His family probably looked a bit like this:

FATHER SPARTACUS, ON HORSEBACK LIKE THE HEROES OF THRACIAN LEGEND

MOTHER SPARTACUS, TATTOOS – VERY MUCH THE FASHION FOR THRACIAN LADIES

BABY SPARTACUS, STARTING HIS TRAINING YOUNG

FAMILY SNAKE – USED BY THRACIANS TO KEEP HOUSEHOLD FREE OF RATS AND MICE. (ALSO IMPORTANT RELIGIOUS SYMBOL OF NATURE)

Young men in the Maidoi made a living looking after sheep and cattle so Spartacus probably spent his early years as a shepherd. It wasn't a very glamorous job, but back then it could be pretty dangerous. Thracian woods (and there were a lot of them) were full of wild animals such as wolves and bears.

These animals weren't fussy if they ate shepherd or sheep, so Spartacus would have been taught how to defend himself. He would have learned to ride and hunt with a spear like the heroes of Thracian legends. He would have practised archery and learned how to use a sling. But most of all, Spartacus would have been skilled in using traditional Thracian weapons – a short curved sword with a small shield. He would have had plenty of time to practise while looking after the sheep. And it would all be excellent training for the future…

During the long days and nights watching over the family flock, Spartacus must have wondered what his future held. He would have grown up listening to his parents telling heroic tales from Maidoi history and about the great battles they had fought when the Macedonians (Thrace's next door neighbours) invaded.

Spartacus probably couldn't write but if he could have he might have scratched out something like this on the ground:

Maidoi Woods, Thrace, 75 BC

I'm bored, bored, bored, bored, bored. Sheep, sheep, sheep, sheep, sheep that's all I ever see. There's not much call for action around here. Even the wolves and bears don't fancy a scrap – I'm big enough to scare them off as soon as they see me.

• Besides, no one ever tells great tales of heroic shepherds. I bet the ancient heroes never had to put up with a bunch of bleating sheep for weeks on end. I wonder if I'll ever get the chance to fight in a big battle? I quite fancy my

11

chances. I reckon I could hold my own in a fight, especially if I had something worth fighting for (and I don't mean protecting a bunch of stupid sheep). What I need is a plan for the future, something to get me out of this woolly work...

But Spartacus would get his chance to make his dreams a reality sooner than he thought. You see, sheep, wolves and bears weren't the only ones who were roaming around Thrace at that time. The country was also full of Romans.

The Romans were a bunch of city types from Italy. Five hundred years before Spartacus's time they had got rid of their king and declared the city of Rome a republic. This meant that the Roman people could rule themselves (as long as they weren't slaves, women, foreigners, peasants or anything like that).

Not content with just running their own city, the Romans gradually conquered the rest of Italy. Then they went on to fight pretty much everyone else who got in their way. By the time Spartacus was a young man, the Romans were well on their way to conquering most of Europe, parts of Africa and the Middle East.

And everywhere the Romans went, they used the same tried-and-tested method to claim new territories for their expanding empire:

Six steps to empire

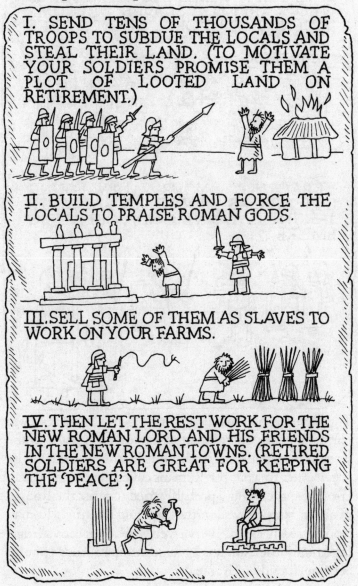

I. SEND TENS OF THOUSANDS OF TROOPS TO SUBDUE THE LOCALS AND STEAL THEIR LAND. (TO MOTIVATE YOUR SOLDIERS PROMISE THEM A PLOT OF LOOTED LAND ON RETIREMENT.)

II. BUILD TEMPLES AND FORCE THE LOCALS TO PRAISE ROMAN GODS.

III. SELL SOME OF THEM AS SLAVES TO WORK ON YOUR FARMS.

IV. THEN LET THE REST WORK FOR THE NEW ROMAN LORD AND HIS FRIENDS IN THE NEW ROMAN TOWNS. (RETIRED SOLDIERS ARE GREAT FOR KEEPING THE 'PEACE'.)

13

V. AFTER A WHILE LET THE LOCALS WHO AREN'T SLAVES BECOME 'FRIENDS' OF ROME. (THAT'S NICE ISN'T IT?)

VI. RECRUIT YOUR NEW-FOUND 'FRIENDS' AS TROOPS, REPEAT STEPS 1-5 UNTIL YOU'VE GOT A GREAT BIG EMPIRE.

The Romans had invaded Thrace before Spartacus was born. The part where Spartacus lived was turned into a Roman province (a territory run by the Romans). The rest was left to what the Romans called 'barbarian' tribes. For a time the Maidoi probably tried to resist the Roman invasion but pretty soon they gave up fighting. (Roman troops really were very, very good at invading.) Eventually the Romans convinced Spartacus's tribe to become 'friends' of Rome.

When in Rome: Barbarians

The Romans considered themselves to be very civilized. They could read and write. They had their own language (called Latin). They built the best buildings around, with central heating and baths. As far as the Romans were concerned, people who still lived in tribes and hadn't learnt to build things like baths were brutal, uncivilized and smelly. The Greeks named these people 'barbarians' because when they spoke it sounded like all they could say was 'barbar'. The Romans thought that was an excellent word and used it to describe most of the peoples of Europe and Persia (modern-day Iran).

For tribes like the Maidoi, being friendly with Rome had its advantages. The Romans would protect them from any local enemies and let them sell their sheep in Rome. But most important of all, the Romans were nice to their 'friends' and tended to kill their enemies or sell them into slavery. Very good reasons indeed to be friendly to the foreigners!

Career opportunities

Every year Rome's 'friends' were required to supply their Italian masters with soldiers. As a young man Spartacus may have seen something like this posted up in his village:

15

LUCULLUS'S AUXILIARIES - LOOKING FOR LADS TO JOIN THE WINNING TEAM!

TRAVEL THE WORLD, MEET NEW PEOPLE - AND KILL THEM. ROME'S WORLD-CLASS ARMY IS LOOKING FOR AUXILIARIES TO WORK UNDER LUCIUS LICINIUS LUCULLUS. ARMOUR AND TRAINING SUPPLIED. GOOD PAY AND LAND-SEIZURE OPPORTUNITIES.

Lucius Licinius Lucullus
ROMAN GENERAL

P.S. IN AGREEMENT WITH THE MAIDOI'S TREATY WITH ROME IT HAS BEEN DECIDED 500 LUCKY LADS SHOULD JOIN THE AUXILIARIES. IF THERE ARE NOT ENOUGH VOLUNTEERS THEN ROME WILL FORCIBLY RECRUIT UNTIL THE 500 PLACES ARE FILLED.

More often than not young men like Spartacus jumped at the chance to join the 'winning team'. In fact, it would have been a pretty good career move for the young Spartacus. Roman troops were better paid, better motivated, better equipped and better trained than the armies they faced. For Spartacus, the army provided the perfect opportunity to escape his boring life as a shepherd and see the world. He was ready to prove himself in battle – just like the Thracian heroes he'd heard so much about…

Lucullus's camp: Somewhere near the Black Sea. 74 BC

This is great! Me and the boys from Thrace are camped out with the Roman army. In just a few hours we built this spectacular camp, it's got walls, tents and proper streets running through it and everything. To be honest it's better built than the village back home. The Prefect who's in charge of us says once we've learnt to camp properly we can start to learn how to fight like the Romans do. Can't wait!

I reckon the Romans are all right. OK, they're a bit snooty with us 'provincials' and they get the plum places in the camp. But I reckon once they see us fight they'll like us a whole lot more. They did say if I joined the Auxiliaries I'd meet people from around the world and they were right. So far I've met Greeks, Egyptians and a load of Spaniards. They're a pretty fearsome bunch. Luckily they're all on the Roman side as well. Don't much fancy the chances of anyone WE run into!

17

Around the time Spartacus joined the Roman army a war broke out. In 74 BC an Asian king, Mithridates VI, was causing trouble. He'd already fought two wars against the Romans. Ten years earlier he'd invaded Greece and Roman Asia (where he'd killed 80,000 Italians who happened to be living there). The Romans didn't think that was on so they kicked him out. Then they decided to cut mischievous Mithridates down to size by seizing some of his own land. They sent Lucius Licinius Lucullus (have you tried saying that quickly three times in a row?) to capture Mithridates and grab some more land on the Black Sea coast. Once Mithridates had finished wondering why Lucullus's parents hadn't got past the letter 'L' in the alphabet, he raised his army. So, for a third time, Mithridates and Rome went to war. For our young Thracian shepherd this was to be his first taste of battle...

🌿 The Legion 🌿

LUCKY LUCULLUS'S WALKOVER
MITHRIDATES' HORDES
VS. ROMAN CUNNING

The battle began with a huge charge by Mithridates' hordes. Obviously they hoped to sweep the legionaries away with a fierce opening move. Things looked bleak for the plucky young lads from Rome, outnumbered ten to one.

However, the barbarians hadn't counted on Roman cunning. On command a defensive hailstorm of javelins went up from the young men of Rome. The spears pinned many barbarians to the ground. Others were forced to throw away their shields as the spears weighed them down. Without their shields the barbarians were an easy target for our fine lancers. Hundreds were cut down.

The enemy retreated and there was a short break. The second half of the battle was less one-sided. Mithridates abandoned the full-frontal assault tactic that had failed so spectacularly in the first half. Sneakily, he split his army and attempted to surround the Romans. The strategy almost worked, but the danger was quickly spotted. Disaster was averted after the legion executed a quick about-face, formed a new battle line and advanced, spears facing front.

Dozens of barbarians were skewered. Several hundred bled to death in front of the Romans. Those that were left were quickly cut down to size with some short-sword work.

In the post-battle interview General Lucullus was generous in victory.

'They got what was coming to them. The barbarians should know they will never defeat the might of Lucullus and his legions!' he said.

So, Lucky Lucullus beat Mithridates and grabbed some more land for the Romans. But General Lucullus wasn't just lucky – he had trained his troops to win using an exhausting daily timetable. Spartacus would have been expected to train every day, learning how to:

19

Spartacus was finding out that the Roman legions didn't win because they were braver than the opposition (they weren't). They won because they had better weapons, discipline and tactics than their enemies had. Roman commanders needed to be sure their soldiers would respond to an order even if it was given in the heat of battle. To make sure they did, the Romans used harsh punishments to keep their troops in line. These ranged from being given food that had gone off to being put to death. Crucifixion was common. So were desertions.

When in Rome: Crucifixion

The Romans were an imaginative bunch when it came to killing. Crucifixion was one of their favourite execution techniques. The victim's forearms were nailed to a plank of wood. Then the plank was hoisted on top of another piece of wood, stuck in the ground. The victim's feet were then nailed to that. Despite losing blood the victim could live for several days before dying of either thirst or suffocation (eventually the victim would become too weak to breathe).

Spartacus might have enjoyed the training and the tactics, but life in the Auxiliaries was tough. Living this close to the Romans the Thracian was finding out what a brutal bunch they could be...

Lucullus's camp: Somewhere in Asia, 74BC

It's all very well doing this training and getting stuck into a good battle but these Romans are starting to get on my nerves. Not only do they keep dishing out stupid punishments (and pretty rank food) but all they do is complain that the war is dragging on and that they don't get paid enough. To make money they keep raiding villages, kidnapping the locals and selling them as slaves. These guys use slaves for EVERYTHING! Tonight I was talking to one soldier who was boasting that his family owned 3,000 of them. They work the family land, cook the food and even help his family get dressed! I'm beginning to wonder if the Romans are worth fighting for at all. The worst thing is they expect me to help round up these poor defenceless peasants. I don't mind fighting to the death in a glorious battle but picking on a bunch of women and children is a bit much. I'm fairly certain that's not the way a hero is supposed to act.

I'm miles from home and I really miss it. I wonder how the sheep are getting on without me?

Of course, Spartacus would have known that the Romans grabbed slaves in the lands they invaded, including Thrace. But this was probably the first time he'd seen first-hand how ruthless the Romans were when they seized innocent people for their slave markets. People were rounded up and shackled together. Slave traders arrived and the people were loaded on to carts to be taken to the slave markets. It must have made quite an impression on our young Thracian hero.

When in Rome: Slaves

For the great majority of Roman slaves life was backbreaking, brutal and brief. They could be sold at any time, beaten or sent to their deaths on the whim of their masters. Slaves were occasionally granted their freedom. If they did something their master really liked or if they'd been faithful servants for a long time, a slave owner might free them in his will.

Leaving the army

Sick of taking orders, bad food and rounding up slaves for the Romans, Spartacus decided to desert from the army. It's also possible that Spartacus wanted to leave so he could get married – we know he got married at some point to a 'prophetess' – a woman who claimed she could see into the future. Running away wasn't a decision a Roman soldier took lightly. If found, he faced a fearsome fate. If he was lucky he might be sold into slavery. If he was unlucky…

It's not known how long Spartacus spent on the run, but it seems Spartacus was one of the 'lucky' ones. About a year later, in early 73 BC, he and his wife were captured and sent to one of the slave markets in Rome. The night before they went up for sale, they were locked up in a cell beneath the market…

Rome, 73 BC

Something really weird happened last night. I was asleep in the slave cell next to the wife, when I began to dream about something slithering around my head. Woke with a start (and a headache) to find my head

24

being squeezed by a large snake. My
wife says this is a sign that I'm soon
going to have tremendous and
fearsome power, but it will all end
horribly. What a comfort she is -
always looking on the bright side of life.

Slave market today. Hope me and the
wife get sold to the same place. I hope
I don't get sold as a city slave. They
get worked to death building roads,
bridges and temples. How I miss a bit
of fresh air and a herd of animals to
look after - a nice quiet life for me
and the wife, that's what I'm after.

ROME STINKS!

Spartacus's wife was right about her husband – he
certainly wasn't destined for a quiet life. He would soon
become powerful, but it would come at a price…

Rome, 73 BC   FREE THE SLAVES (AND THEIR WIVES!)

Forced to stand in a market all
morning. There were hundreds of us
from all over the place. These
people prodded us and checked our
teeth like we were a herd of

ROME STINKS! so do you!

25

cattle. That's about all we are to them.

At lunchtime this rich Roman came up to the slave market. He asked me to lift a basket of rocks. (Which I did easily.) Then he asked if I had any military training. I didn't answer until forced to by the salesman. (Those whips can be pretty convincing.)

'Yes, plenty,' I growled in my gruffest voice.

'Oh good,' he replied, 'I'll take him, that woman and two of the Gauls.'

'Phew,' I thought. 'At least the wife's coming with me.'

But it wasn't good news. Imagine how you'd feel then when the man turns round to you and says: 'Cheer up, you're all going to gladiator school...'

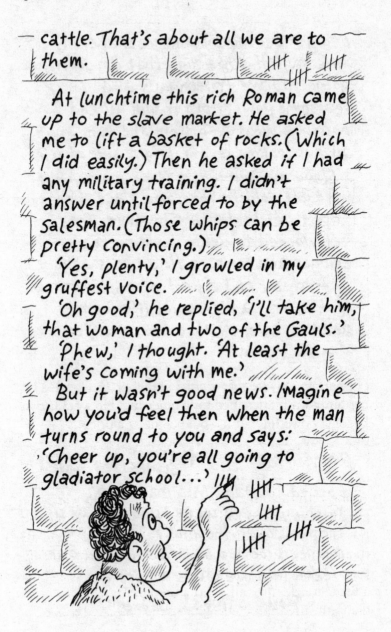

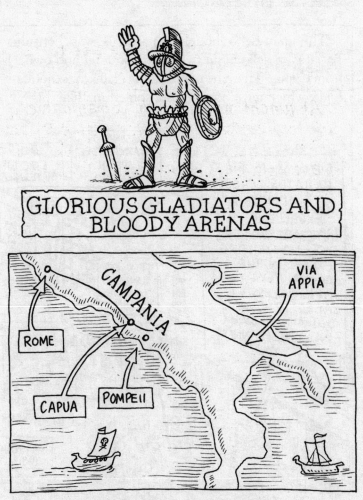

GLORIOUS GLADIATORS AND BLOODY ARENAS

Along with the other slaves, Spartacus and his wife were put into a caged cart with little or no protection from the hot sun. Armed guards escorted the captives, ready to kill them if they made an attempt to get away. Occasionally each slave would be allowed to drink a little water and eat a little bread. After all, there's no point buying slaves to die in the arena and letting them die on a road.

The man who bought Spartacus was Lentulus Batiatus, a rich *lanista* (a gladiator trainer and owner) from Capua. There he owned a big gladiator school, or *Ludo*, which must have looked something like this:

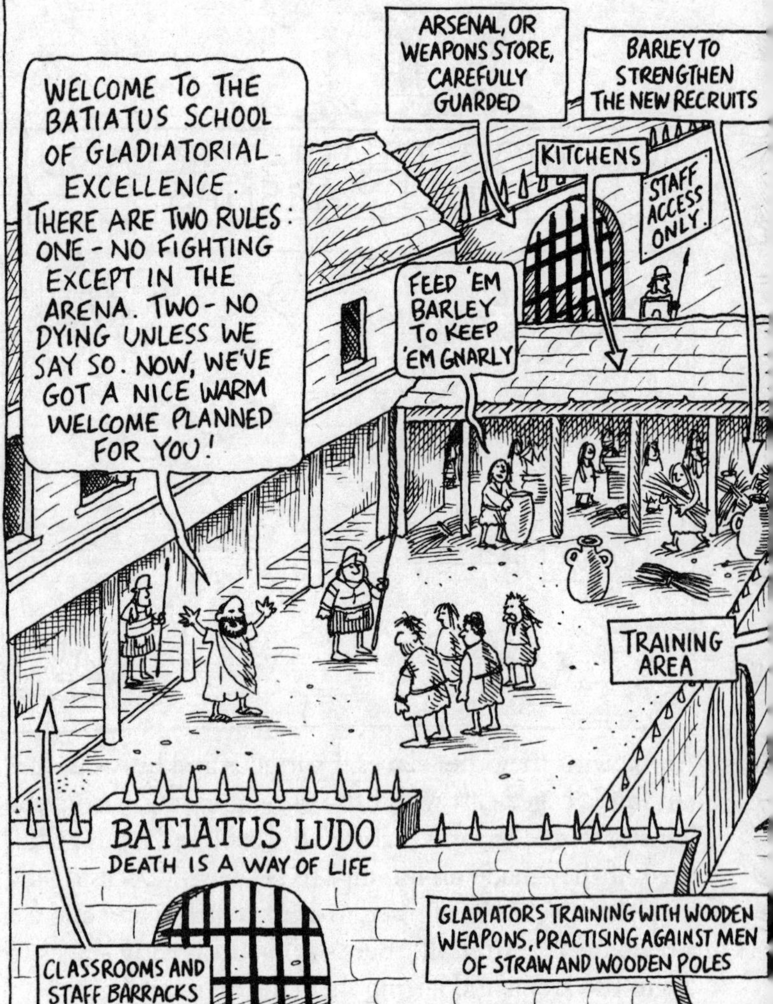

ARSENAL, OR WEAPONS STORE, CAREFULLY GUARDED

BARLEY TO STRENGTHEN THE NEW RECRUITS

KITCHENS

STAFF ACCESS ONLY

WELCOME TO THE BATIATUS SCHOOL OF GLADIATORIAL EXCELLENCE. THERE ARE TWO RULES: ONE - NO FIGHTING EXCEPT IN THE ARENA. TWO - NO DYING UNLESS WE SAY SO. NOW, WE'VE GOT A NICE WARM WELCOME PLANNED FOR YOU!

FEED 'EM BARLEY TO KEEP 'EM GNARLY

TRAINING AREA

BATIATUS LUDO — DEATH IS A WAY OF LIFE

CLASSROOMS AND STAFF BARRACKS

GLADIATORS TRAINING WITH WOODEN WEAPONS, PRACTISING AGAINST MEN OF STRAW AND WOODEN POLES

You might have your name written on the label of your PE kit in case it gets lost. Well, at the Ludo, they did the same thing, only the labels were permanent. Spartacus and his fellow slaves were all branded with Batiatus's name (a specially shaped red-hot poker was pressed against their flesh). That way if any of them escaped whoever caught them would know who to return them to.

After their 'welcome', Spartacus and the other new arrivals were taken down to the barracks. By locking the gladiators underground every night Batiatus and his training staff hoped to prevent any breakout, but it didn't stop Spartacus and his fellow slaves dreaming of it...

—Batiatus's Ludo, 73 BC —

"Terrible first day. They're a tough lot, these gladiator trainers. To top it all, the wife says that the only way out of here is to die in the arena. I swear she says things like that just to wind me up. When I

30

mentioned what she'd said to Crixus – he's the Gaul in the next cell – he said, 'She's right, Spartacus, but you and I will escape before then.' But there's no way we can escape at the moment. We're under constant guard. Crixus needs to learn patience. It's no good trying to break out until we've got a really good plan. I'll sleep on it and see what I can come up with...

Gladiator school

By the time Spartacus was sold to Batiatus the arena had become part and parcel of Roman life. Rich Romans who wanted to become politicians would pay good money to put on spectacular shows. By giving the poorer Roman citizens the chance to see gory games they hoped to win their votes. Romans wanting the best gladiators for their games came to Capua to buy them. With just a few months' training a slave like Spartacus would fetch several times what Batiatus had paid for him.

Glad to be a gladiator?
Gladiators were originally known as *bustuarii* – funeral men. At first, Romans made a pair of slaves or criminals fight each other to the death at funerals. The loser became a sacrifice to the dead

31

person. Then, to make things more exciting, the fighters were trained in special schools and became known as gladiators. People liked the fights so much that they began to use any excuse to stage them: weddings, anniversaries, birthdays, market days, Mondays, Tuesdays, Wednesdays…

Thousands flocked to see gladiators slaughter each other at the arena and the fans followed the games like some people follow football. But instead of win, lose or draw, the arena had its own sinister scoring system:

Some gladiators were so good at winning that they became famous and were adored by their fans. If they won enough fights, they could even be set free. But winning wasn't easy and their training needed to be tough. At Batiatus's school, Spartacus would probably have had a training timetable to follow. The Roman day was divided into 12 equal segments between sunrise and sunset, and the training sessions would have been divided up accordingly. Spartacus's school timetable may have looked something like this:

BATIATUS'S SCHOOL OF GLADIATORIAL EXCELLENCE
~

Name: **Spartacus of Thrace**

(hours after sunrise)

Time	Lesson	Notes
I (cock crow)	General fitness. Running, lifting and stretching. *Sigh*	Running round a track can get a bit boring. Mind you, if they did let us out I reckon we'd run a lot faster... away from here.
II	Light breakfast *Yuk!*	Barley. The wife's working in the kitchens, I'll have a word, see if she can't get us some fruit.
III	Sword and dagger drills. How to use a sword to cut, thrust and block.	It's just like old times in Lucullus's army...
IV	Lunch	Apparently barley builds up muscle (I guess puny gladiators don't make for good shows). That must

Time	Lesson	Notes
	Yuk	be why we're sometimes called 'barley men'...
V	Arena etiquette How to kill and how to die in the arena. *Sorry about that* *not at all*	If these Romans really want to see some killing they should join the legions. At least then they wouldn't have to get us lot to do it for them.
VI VII	Speciality combat (double lesson) *grrr!* *roar*	Practised yet another historic battle that we're expected to recreate for the Roman crowds. Then we had animal hunting and fighting. We're up against bears, wolves and leopards – this is worse than being back home!
VIII	General fitness *boring*	Enough of this already! I'm starting to ache. (Still, we're fit enough to make a run for it when we get a chance.)

Time	Lesson	Notes
IX	Dinner *barf*	Barley again – barf-ley more like.
X	Sword and dagger drills	Me and Crixus are the best in the class at this. The trainers are lucky they only let us use wooden swords... If we ever get our hands on the real thing they'd better watch it.
XI	Arena procedure *Jolly nice tea* *Super!*	All this talking about manners and rules in the arena: it's a fight to the death, not a tea party!
XII	Massage, bathing and appearance *Sigh!*	Are they serious? Apparently the fans expect us to look good while killing (and dying) in the arena. Still, it's a great chance to relax...

35

Gory glory

As part of his arena procedure class, Spartacus would have had to learn the four gladiator virtues:

The noble citizens of Rome held these virtues dear. If slaves and criminals, like Spartacus, lived by them then they too must be able to follow the code. In fact some Romans even volunteered to fight in the arena. They had to take an oath:

I PROMISE TO BE BURNT WITH FIRE, SHACKLED WITH CHAINS, WHIPPED WITH RODS AND KILLED WITH STEEL...

So far, Spartacus had been burnt with fire (branded), shackled with chains and whipped with rods. He was in no hurry to be killed with steel as well. But unlike the Roman volunteers Spartacus and his school friends didn't have a choice. They were at the Batiatus School to learn, and if they didn't, they would die. (Even if they did learn they would die anyway.)

As well as the four virtues, Spartacus also had to learn the rules of the arena:

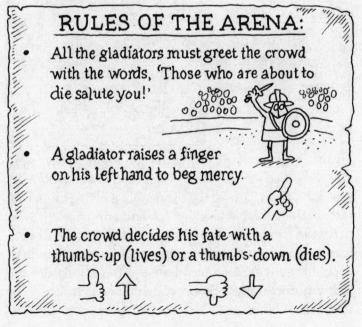

RULES OF THE ARENA:

- All the gladiators must greet the crowd with the words, 'Those who are about to die salute you!'

- A gladiator raises a finger on his left hand to beg mercy.

- The crowd decides his fate with a thumbs-up (lives) or a thumbs-down (dies).

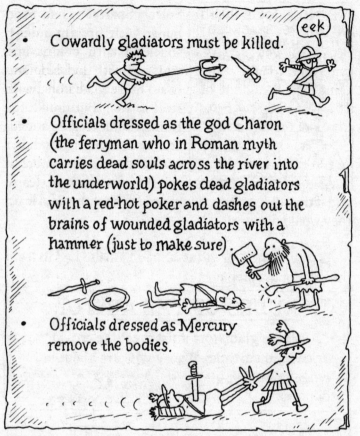

- Cowardly gladiators must be killed.

- Officials dressed as the god Charon (the ferryman who in Roman myth carries dead souls across the river into the underworld) pokes dead gladiators with a red-hot poker and dashes out the brains of wounded gladiators with a hammer (just to make sure).

- Officials dressed as Mercury remove the bodies.

Gladiator games didn't only entertain Romans, they were also seen as educational. (You can thank your lucky stars that 'educational' these days generally means a bit boring rather than very bloody!) In ancient times it was necessary for everyone to be ready to fight. Some Roman leaders worried that ordinary people wouldn't be able to cope if they had to go into battle. After all, battles are pretty horrid things. Blood and carnage can turn your stomach and can turn the best soldiers into cowards.

From the safety of their seats in the arena Romans were prepared for the gore they might encounter on the battlefield. The fighters were often named after people who had fought (and lost) against the Romans (Thracians being one of them). These gladiators, with their own styles of fighting and weapons, prepared the crowd for the different people they might meet in battle.

At gladiator school, Spartacus would have had to learn several different styles of fighting. In fact, he probably made notes on the main ones in his schoolbook…

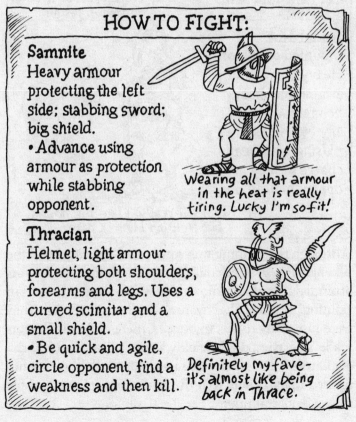

HOW TO FIGHT:

Samnite
Heavy armour protecting the left side; stabbing sword; big shield.
• Advance using armour as protection while stabbing opponent.

Wearing all that armour in the heat is really tiring. Lucky I'm so fit!

Thracian
Helmet, light armour protecting both shoulders, forearms and legs. Uses a curved scimitar and a small shield.
• Be quick and agile, circle opponent, find a weakness and then kill.

Definitely my fave - it's almost like being back in Thrace.

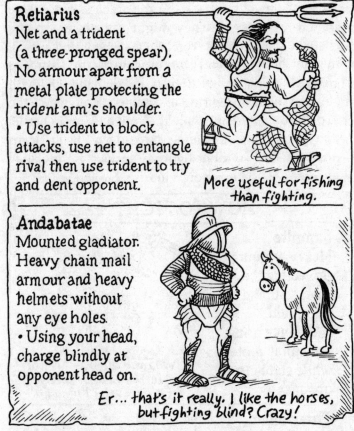

Retiarius
Net and a trident
(a three-pronged spear).
No armour apart from a
metal plate protecting the
trident arm's shoulder.
• Use trident to block
attacks, use net to entangle
rival then use trident to try
and dent opponent.

More useful for fishing
than fighting.

Andabatae
Mounted gladiator.
Heavy chain mail
armour and heavy
helmets without
any eye holes.
• Using your head,
charge blindly at
opponent head on.

Er... that's it really. I like the horses,
but fighting blind? Crazy!

Although the training was very harsh, Spartacus and the
other gladiators were comparatively well treated. Doctors
attended to gladiators when they were injured in
training. (Unless they were so badly injured that they
were just going to die anyway. In these cases the doctors
made sure they died quickly.) As well as doctors, the
gladiators were given massages. After all, the coaches
needed to make sure that the gladiators remained supple
after a day's training.

Glad to be a gladiator?
For well over 1,000 years our knowledge of the human body came from gladiators. A Greek physician called Galen worked as a gladiator doctor. He used the deep cuts and wounds of the gladiators to poke around inside and take notes. He discovered that arteries carry blood and his diagram of a human heart was still being studied by doctors in the sixteenth century.

INTERESTING...

Fighting friends

As Spartacus spent more and more time at Batiatus's school he began to make friends. This was no mean feat. The gladiators were expressly forbidden from talking (although yelling abuse in the arena was encouraged). At mealtimes the guards stopped any 'unnecessary' conversations. When they *were* free to speak the gladiators generally spoke in different languages. Then for the rest of the day the gladiators were being taught to fight and kill one another. Certainly not the best state of affairs to make friends.

None the less, Spartacus did make some good friends at Batiatus's school. As they came to the end of their training, Spartacus and his mates began to feel like real gladiators: ready to face the world together...

But for Spartacus and his comrades-in-arms there was no escaping one simple fact. They were literally being fattened up for the slaughter...

Batiatus's Ludo, 73 BC

This is all very interesting, and I'm enjoying all the keeping fit, weapons training and the massages (the food's still terrible though). But I'm not keen on the idea of having to kill for a bunch of Roman 'fans'... and I'm really not keen on dying for them! I'd rather slaughter Romans than my fellow gladiators. What if I have to fight one of my friends? Crixus says not to worry, he'll make sure I die quickly (as if! I'm much better than he is with a sword) but I'd rather we all got out of this alive. I've got to work out how we can all get out of here...

CAPUA GLADIATORS RULE!

THE BIG BREAKFAST BREAKOUT

After months of training and training and more training, Batiatus's new recruits were ready for the arena. Along with Crixus, Castus, Gannicus and Oenomaus, Spartacus would have been put back into the caged cart. It's a fair bet that Batiatus took his gladiators to one of the arenas near Capua. One of the nearest and best of them was in Pompeii.

Set near Mount Vesuvius (at that time a dormant volcano), Pompeii had one of the most modern amphitheatres in Italy (the Old Trafford of the ancient world). Big enough to fit 12,000 bloodthirsty spectators (half the town's population) the amphitheatre was less than ten years old.

There was nothing the people of Pompeii liked more than some good gladiator games. Especially when it featured their local rivals from Capua…

Pompeii Arena, 73 BC

So this is it. We're going to fight – and this time it's for real. Well at least we'll be fighting as a team instead of against each other. Crixus and I have convinced the others to stick close and do what we say… with my military experience and Crixus's rage I reckon we can take Pompeii's team. I'm pretty nervous though, this isn't like fighting in a big battle. At least in a war no one's watching you.

DOWN UR POMPEII!

Spoke to the wife before we left Batiatus's school. She was her usual happy self, saying, 'The only way out of the arena for good is to die, Spartacus.' Well, we're going to live and find another way out, whatever she says!

Capua's gladiators were famous for a reason – the schools there were the best in Italy. Spartacus and his friends were now superbly trained killing machines. With their bravery and skill Spartacus was right to be confident.

The Daily Gladius

HEADS DROPPED!

Final score: Pompeii: 19 Died, 1 Won, 0 Wounded
Capua: 1 Died, 17 Won, 2 Wounded
Man of the Match: Spartacus, Capua

Capua's dominance in the CGL (Campanian Gladiators League) continued yesterday with a devastating display of fighting skills. Despite their new amphitheatre, Pompeii were cut down to size by the silky skills of Capua's gladiators.

12,000 of Pompeii's plebians had packed the place to back their battling brothers in this local derby but it wasn't to be. Batiatus's men were awesome. They soon settled into their usual style of play. Pompeian heads dropped. Literally. Capua's finest put on a display of sword work and spear fighting that would shame the most aggressive legionaries. The Pompeii crowd, always ready to acknowledge technical excellence, cheered the fighters on.

Two in particular deserve special mention: a Thracian called Spartacus and a Gaul called Crixus. At one point five Pompeian fighters surrounded them. It looked bleak for Batiatus's boys. But Spartacus used a fine move to capture a horse from one of his mounted opponents. While Crixus held off the other four, Spartacus was then able to wheel the horse around and slaughter the Pompeians from behind.

On yesterday's form Batiatus's boys could go all the way to Rome and beyond. They showed all the virtues we've come to expect from the Batiatus School. The way they effortlessly despatched Pompeii and fought on despite injuries just shows what heroes they are capable of becoming. Now he's at the top of the league it's only a matter of time before Batiatus finds his way to Rome and greater glory!

THE CGL SPONSORED BY MARS. (ROMAN GOD OF WAR)

A PRAYER TO MARS A DAY HELPS YOU WORK, REST AND SLAY

After the match, the crowd showered the successful (i.e. surviving) gladiators with flowers and wine. They were treated like heroes. Batiatus was convinced that his boys would make it big in Rome.

STICK WITH ME, BOYS, AND I'LL MAKE YOU DEAD FAMOUS!

MAKE US DEAD, MORE LIKE

But Spartacus and his friends knew this glory would be short-lived. Winning a fight meant more fights, more fights meant more killing, more killing meant more glory, which meant more fights. You get the picture. Each time a gladiator stepped into the arena there was a chance he wasn't coming back.

Glad to be a gladiator?
Some slaves went to extraordinary lengths to avoid fighting in the arena. One Roman writer tells of how a German slave killed himself before a fight. The Romans used sticks with a sponge on the end to clean themselves up after going to the loo. This poor slave stuck one down his throat and suffocated himself. Other slaves killed themselves by pushing their heads through the wheels of the carts they travelled in.

The choice for Spartacus was clear. Either die in the arena fighting other slaves or die outside it fighting Romans. And Spartacus wasn't the type of man to die without a fight…

Batiatus's Ludo, 73 BC

I spoke to the wife and she said something bad was going to happen (again!). Normally when she says that it's 'cos the barley's been burnt. But later I spoke to Crixus. He overheard Batiatus striking a deal with some big shot from Rome. We are to be sold for a spectacular show in the city, playing the forces of Carthage that were slaughtered by the Romans years ago. We will surely die. Batiatus has sold us and made himself enough money to buy a new lot of slaves to train.

Crixus says we are to leave the day after tomorrow. 'No chance of escape in Rome, Spartacus, we wouldn't get half a mile out of the city before they cut us down. We must make a break for it now.' For once I agree with him. I've got a plan and the other gladiators are with me on it - they all agree they'd rather take their chances on the open road than in the Roman arena. Our best chance is if we all go at once. The guards won't expect a mass escape. I'll send a note to the wife in the kitchens. She'll help us. She says all the kitchen slaves are as eager to escape as we are. Since the games in Pompeii, Batiatus has let us eat without being shackled. He thinks we're all ready to die for him in Rome. But we're going to cook up a little 'Gladiator Surprise' for him...

49

In the end, 200 gladiators were in on Spartacus's plan. Everything was in place for…

The great escape

ONCE THEY'D LEFT THE SCHOOL GATES, THE GLADIATORS STARTED TO RUN OFF INTO THE COUNTRYSIDE. BUT SPARTACUS'S MILITARY TRAINING TOLD HIM THEY STOOD A BETTER CHANCE OF MAKING A GETAWAY IF THEY STAYED AROUND TO DEFEAT ANY PURSUERS. EXPECTING A RAG-TAG BAND OF ESCAPED SLAVES, BATIATUS'S SOLDIERS RUSHED AFTER THEM PELL-MELL, BUT THE GLADIATORS WERE EXPERT WARRIORS AND THEY WERE FIGHTING FOR THEIR FREEDOM.

I'M SURE THEY'RE SUPPOSED TO BE RUNNING AWAY!

The Romans had swords, shields and javelins while the gladiators were only armed with cooking equipment. But despite the mismatch the gladiators gave the Romans quite a beating. (The first of many.)

The victory came at a high price. Of the 200 that were supposed to have escaped just over 70 gladiators and a few dozen other slaves made it out alive. But those that did so had escaped against huge odds. Never before had so many gladiators escaped from a school in one attempt.

From the defeated garrison, Spartacus and his men took the Roman armour, javelins and swords. Before they left, several of the gladiators set fire to Batiatus's school. As far as they were concerned, its days of gladiator training were over.

As they stood on the road outside Batiatus's school, watching the flames engulf it, the gladiators wondered what would become of them. Even now Batiatus would be reporting the uprising to local Romans. If they waited they would surely be hunted down by a better-armed garrison from Rome. After all, they were only 70 trained men and a few slaves, what could they do against the might of Rome? As the gladiators discussed their situation one voice was heard above the rest.

'Comrades – I think I have a plan…'

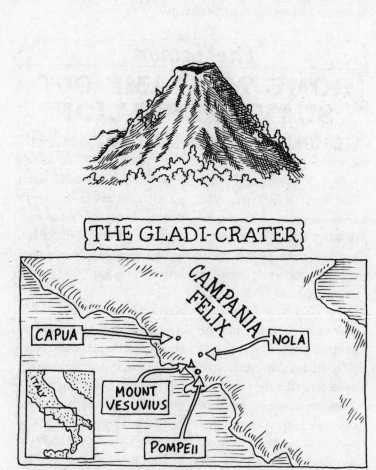

THE GLADI-CRATER

CAPUA

CAMPANIA FELIX

NOLA

ITALY

MOUNT VESUVIUS

POMPEII

Spartacus knew that the Romans would send someone to hunt them down at once. Not only were the gladiators runaway slaves, they'd defeated a garrison of Roman soldiers *and* destroyed the school of Lentulus Batiatus. As if that wasn't enough they were going to have to raid the homes of rich Romans to get food and drink. Romans didn't like runaway slaves and they liked bandits even less. Sure enough, the Romans didn't waste any time when they got the news from Capua...

53

The Legion

ROME TO STAMP OUT SLAVE REBELLION

'GLAD TO KILL GLADIATORS', SAYS CLAUDIUS GLABER

Rome has acted decisively against a group of upstart gladiators from Capua. The up-and-coming magistrate Claudius Glaber, 39, has been asked to recruit 3,000 locals to hunt down the rebel slaves. The senate presented Glaber with a Fasces. This ancient symbol of power will strike fear into the hearts of all who see it.

The dashing magistrate told this reporter that there was little doubt the campaign would be swift and successful: 'The overwhelming might of Rome will quickly put an end to the uprising,' he said. 'We will hunt them down like the dogs they are and put paid to their idea of freedom. I'll nail the 70 gladiators to crosses to make an example of them to the rest of Rome's sorry slaves. How can gladiators hope to be free? By being killed. If they refuse to come and die in the arena then we will have to take the arena to them. I only regret that my troops and I will not be fighting worthy opponents; slaves are such a bore to kill.'

Knives out for Batiatus

After the gladiators are rounded up and destroyed, Batiatus will face an inquiry into the escape. Tough questions regarding gladiator security are already being asked in the senate.

How Rome works

The senate: 600 of Rome's finest nobility chosen by the censors to help rule Rome. Deciding legal, religious and moral questions, these guys are the best of the best.

When in Rome: The Fasces

The city of Rome hadn't become the capital of a world empire without knowing how to punish people. It even had its own symbol of power: the Fasces. Whoever carried the Fasces in front of them  had the right to impose the death penalty (shown by the axe) or just a severe beating (shown by the rods). Two thousand years later a bunch of Italians borrowed the word to become power-mad Fascists.

Meanwhile, outside the gates of Batiatus's burning school, Spartacus was drawing up his next plan. He knew that if the band were to survive they'd need more than 70 gladiators and a handful of kitchen slaves from Batiatus's school. A hundred slaves against the might of Rome? They might as well save the Romans the trouble and nail themselves to the crosses. What they really needed was a hideout. Somewhere the Romans couldn't easily attack them. While he'd been on tour in Pompeii Spartacus had seen just the place…

SPARTACUS DESCRIBED HOW THE MOUNTAIN HAD A HOLLOW CRATER AT THE TOP, IDEAL FOR A BUNCH OF RUNAWAYS TO HIDE IN.

VESUVIUS WAS THE HIGHEST POINT OF LAND FOR MILES AROUND, IDEAL FOR KEEPING WATCH FOR ROMAN LEGIONS.

BEST OF ALL, THE WEALTHY COUNTRYSIDE THAT SURROUNDED THE MOUNTAIN WAS IDEAL FOR LOOTING FOOD AND RICHES.

The slaves and gladiators liked the plan. Besides, it was Spartacus who'd planned the breakout. Why not follow him further? Staying off the road, Spartacus marched his band of followers 30 miles south of Capua into the fertile land near Pompeii.

Pompeii was set in an area of Italy known as the *Campania Felix* or 'happy countryside'. But for rich Romans who took a holiday there in 73 BC the land was anything but 'happy' and their holidays far from relaxing. Instead, the countryside was alive with stories of bandit raids. Villas were vandalized, livestock was looted and riches were robbed. The bandits showed no mercy. They killed rich Romans and freed their slaves. Then they vanished, disappearing into the countryside like the summer rain.

Posters offering rewards for the return of runaway slaves were pasted on every wall. And on them appeared a new and terrifying name…

WANTED
DEAD OR ALIVE.
Escaped slaves from the gladiator school of Lentulus Batiatus

*

REWARDS FOR RETURNED RUNAWAYS:

1 Gold talent for each slain slave
2 Gold talents for each returned alive
3 Gold talents for each gladiator (dead or alive)
4 Gold talents for Spartacus, * leader of the slave scum

For once, the rich Romans were getting a very up-close-and-personal demonstration of gladiator skills. In slave quarters across Campania Spartacus and the gladiators were greater heroes than they could ever have been in the arena. If they found a master who had been particularly nasty to his slaves then the gladiators would be particularly nasty to him. These were gladiators after all; they knew a thing or two about killing with style.

Inside the gladi-crater

As Spartacus had suggested, the gladiators camped out in the crater at the top of Vesuvius. Although there was no water, it was the perfect hiding place.

CRIXUS RETURNING FROM A RAID.

THICK VINES COVERING STEEP SLOPES ON ALL SIDES. STOPS ANYONE CLIMBING UP TO ATTACK THE CAMP.

WHAT A GREAT HIDEOUT. SO MANY VILLAS TO ROB!

59

Spartacus made sure that loot was shared equally among the band of escaped slaves. They had plenty of food and drink and any number of new recruits to take on raids. Life was good in the gladi-crater, so most of the gladiators were quite happy to let things carry on the way they were. But Spartacus was not so sure…

Vesuvius, 73 BC

Everyone agrees it was a good idea of mine to camp out here. They're certainly all enjoying the local facilities.

The wife says it can't last and for once I agree. Eventually the Romans will find us. Whenever I try and raise the question of what we're going to do everyone just talks about which villa they want to attack next. The wife says they're all drunk on freedom (I say it's the wine).

When the Romans find us they're going to be really, really angry. Every time we loot a Roman house all the slaves want to join us. I guess you can't blame them. If they stay there Glaber will probably accuse them of helping us. Then he'll nail them to

crosses. Even if we tell them they
can't join us they follow us and try
to sneak into the camp. It's going to
be harder to escape the more of us
there are.
  Already there are fights breaking out.
Crixus laughs it off (he does like a
good scrap!) and says, 'Gladiators will
be gladiators, Spartacus.' But I'm
worried. If we can't get on together
when there's only a few hundred of
us what chance have we got when
there's more than that?
  What we need is another plan. That'd
stop everyone fussing and fighting.

Spartacus was now dealing with a lot more people than the hundred or so that had escaped from Batiatus's school. Within weeks the camp had doubled, then tripled in size. The Gauls and Thracians and Germans and Spanish and Greeks and Africans all had their separate areas of the camp. There they collected around the fires, sang songs of home and worshipped their own gods. Arguments flared up between the different nationalities. The gladiators tried to keep the newcomers from fighting each other by sharing all the loot equally but it was a tough job.

  Eventually everyone realized they needed a leader to deal with all the problems. A big meeting was called so that everyone could have their say. Clearly the gladiators were the most likely candidates for leadership (they were the leaders of the original breakout after all, and they also happened to be the best fighters). But which one would they choose?

CASTUS

PLAN
- GET EVERYONE TOGETHER AND START MARCHING NORTH TO GAUL. "IT'S A LOVELY PLACE AND I WANT TO GO HOME..."

QUALIFICATIONS
- ONE OF THE ORIGINAL GLADIATORS
- STRONG AND FEARLESS

GAUL for ALL!

CRIXUS

PLAN
- CONTINUE LOOTING AND PILLAGING
- USE FIGHTING SKILLS TO KILL ROMANS (AND ANYONE ELSE WHO GETS IN THE WAY)
- "MARCH ON ROME!"

QUALIFICATIONS
- BRILLIANT GLADIATOR
- SUPPORTED BY MOST OF THE GAULS IN THE CAMP (EXCEPT FOR CASTUS)
- VERY, VERY SCARY WHEN ANGRY

REVENGE REVENGE REVENGE

The Thracians in the camp and the slaves who had joined them since Capua voted overwhelmingly for Spartacus. Some of the Gauls also voted for him but many voted for Crixus. To prevent a split in the camp it was decided that Spartacus would be appointed leader with Crixus, Castus and Oenomaus acting as his lieutenants. Crixus wasn't too happy about this but the decision was made.

Now the slaves could turn their minds to more pressing matters...

Escape from Vesuvius

Claudius Glaber had raised his 3,000 men and finally made his way to Campania. After trying (and failing) to catch the rebel slaves in the open Glaber eventually discovered their hiding place on Vesuvius. Full of Roman confidence and pride Glaber at first tried sending his troops to take the camp. (Of course he stayed at the bottom of the mountain urging them on. After all, important Romans like himself shouldn't get involved in the dangerous business of fighting runaway slaves. That's what the soldiers were for.) But Glaber's confidence was misplaced...

Those Romans that did make it to the top were tired out and no match for the gladiators standing guard at the crater's entrance. After a day of trying to rush the slave camp Glaber gave up. His men were mainly old soldiers and farmers from the countryside. They had joined up to hunt a bunch of runaway slaves to earn a bit of extra money. They hadn't joined up to die. After throwing themselves against the well-guarded crater they quickly became thoroughly disheartened.

Instead of trying to take the crater by force Glaber hit on another tactic. He would starve them out. So Glaber ordered his men to set up camp across the pathway just out of reach of any rocks or boulders the slaves might throw at them.

Water torture

Inside the slave camp the situation became desperate. The slaves had plenty of food. The real problem was water. Without water the slaves could only last a few days. In the hot sun in the dry volcano crater their thirst must have been terrible.

For some of the slaves it must have been too much. Some sneaked away from the camp and ran back to the Romans begging for forgiveness and a drink. The Romans gave them a quick sip of water before slitting their throats. To Glaber these slaves were proof that he would soon crush the gladiators and the slave uprising. He sat in his tent at night, eating, drinking and thinking of the glory that would be his when he returned to Rome.

The volcano erupts

As Glaber gloated, the gladiators gathered. They couldn't stay trapped in the crater for ever. It looked bad for them, but Spartacus was not about to let a bunch of sub-standard soldiers defeat him that easily.

Quickly, he called his lieutenants to a meeting and outlined his plan to get out.

Claudius Glaber hadn't set up camp properly. Since the Romans were confident the slaves would never attack their camp they saw little need for digging their usual ditch and fortified wall. Of course, this was fine while Spartacus was cooped up in the crater but when the slaves charged the camp it led to all kinds of confusion.

Roman officers tried to rally their men but didn't know exactly where they were. Soon they were all only obeying one order…

Within minutes the Roman camp had fallen to Spartacus's followers. After posting sentries around the camp's perimeter Spartacus and his commanders met in the centre. Claudius Glaber was nowhere to be found (he'd run away back to Rome as fast as he could). So Spartacus's gang made use of the Roman camp. They ate the food, drank the water and slept in the tents of the men Rome had sent to kill them.

Spartacus probably took Glaber's tent for himself.

Vesuvius, Glaber's tent, 73 BC

Everyone's really chuffed after this morning's battle. Crixus and the guys say they haven't enjoyed a fight that much since the big breakfast breakout. Every time I poke my head out of the tent they all cheer and say, 'Hail, Spartacus! The Man with the Plan!' I love it when a plan comes together!

Our new camp is great. It's much better than the old one. Not only does it have water, food and the latest in tent technology but the Romans very thoughtfully left us loads of weapons and armour. I even found some nice paper to write my diary on. No more scratching around on the ground! And that's not all we've found. Glaber was in such a hurry to leave that he abandoned his fasces. It was left lying in the dirt. I think I'll use it later. Maybe we'll carry it in front of us when we start marching. Their symbol of power carried by the very man it was supposed to have broken? They won't like that in Rome!

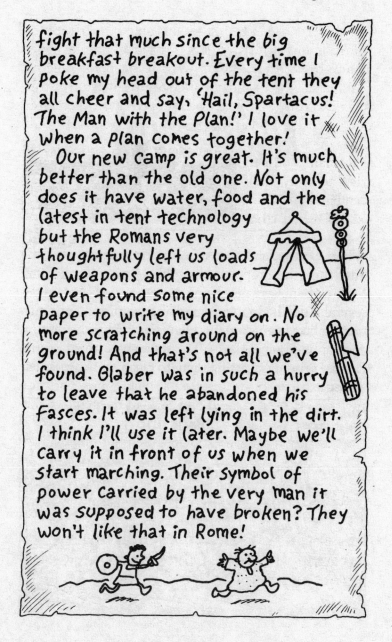

THE THREE THUGS

When Glaber made his getaway the Fasces wasn't the only thing he dropped. His soldiers were left behind. Most of them were now being carried out to be buried but several dozen had survived and were being held prisoner. Glaber had been carrying chains and whips to use on any captured rebel slaves. The slaves used them on the Roman prisoners, getting them to clean up the mess left after the battle.

The slaves laughed and joked as they made the Romans work in the hot sun. They'd been the ones who had to work in chain gangs. Now they were the ones watching. Just a few days ago they'd been starving and dying of thirst. Now they were full of good food and wine. The slaves must have found it all very funny.

But back in Rome, Claudius Glaber wasn't laughing…

☙ The Legion ❧

GLOOMY GLABER'S SHOCK DEFEAT

Claudius Glaber has returned to Rome in disgrace. News quickly spread that Glaber had been defeated by a ragtag bunch of slaves at the foot of Mount Vesuvius. Most of his 3,000 soldiers are missing presumed dead.

As Glaber made his way to the senate to deliver his report dressed in his nightshirt, citizens lined the street and yelled insults. 'He couldn't catch a cold, let alone a slave,' said one man. 'We'll have to call him Gloomy Glaber from now on,' said another.

'I almost died out there.'
The senators also gave Glaber a harsh reception. Glaber told the senate he had been abandoned by his soldiers and had fought for hours on his own before making a tactical retreat. One senator then asked why reports from other survivors described Glaber running from the scene of battle at the first opportunity. 'They are mistaken,' said Glaber. 'I fought as any man would fight.' 'In your nightshirt?' asked the senator. When the other senators had stopped laughing, Glaber

replied, 'It's not funny, I almost died out there.'

The senate has now sacked Glaber and sent another magistrate, Varinius, against the slaves. The senators, furious at Glaber's failure, have also sent the well-known magistrates Furius and Cossinius with 2,000 men each. They have vowed to regain the Fasces and make the slaves pay for humiliating the power of Rome.

The prisoner question

When the Roman prisoners had finished cleaning the camp, the slaves and gladiators discussed what to do with them. Spartacus, Crixus and Castus all had different ideas…

KILL 'EM ALL! NAIL 'EM TO CROSSES! THAT'LL MAKE THE ROMANS THINK TWICE BEFORE CROSSING US AGAIN!

NO, TAKE THEIR WEAPONS AND LET THEM GO!

NO, NO! KILL SOME OF THEM AND LET THE OTHERS GO. THAT WAY THE ROMANS WILL KNOW WE MEAN BUSINESS!

Some of the slaves agreed with Crixus. After all, these men had joined Glaber to hunt them down and kill them. Why not take revenge, or at least follow Castus's advice? But Spartacus was thinking longer-term. If they killed Glaber's men the Romans would be able to recruit more locals looking for revenge. If they let the Romans

72

go it would show the locals that the slaves were more civilized than the Romans. Winter was coming and Spartacus knew that the former slaves would soon be depending on local towns to feed them.

Crixus and Castus had a lot of support. But since the defeat of Glaber's troops, Spartacus had reached new heights of popularity in the slave camp. His idea of a sneak attack on Glaber's camp was seen as a military masterpiece. And not just by his slave followers. As news spread that the fearless gladiator Spartacus had defeated a Roman army, more and more people flocked to join the uprising.

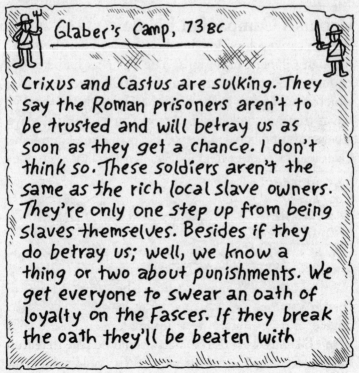

Glaber's Camp, 73 BC

Crixus and Castus are sulking. They say the Roman prisoners aren't to be trusted and will betray us as soon as they get a chance. I don't think so. These soldiers aren't the same as the rich local slave owners. They're only one step up from being slaves themselves. Besides if they do betray us; well, we know a thing or two about punishments. We get everyone to swear an oath of loyalty on the Fasces. If they break the oath they'll be beaten with

rods and killed with an axe.
Crixus and Castus say it's not fair
that I always get my own way. The
wife says they're jealous. She says I
need to find them something to do
or they'll start causing mischief.
Well, we're going to need more
food and provisions so I'll send them
out to get food. That ought to
keep them busy...

Crixus's Campanian holiday

It hadn't taken long for the slave gang to eat their way
through Glaber's provisions. The Romans had stocked
enough food to last an army of 3,000 several weeks,
which would have been more than enough for the 100
slaves that originally escaped from Capua. But the slave
rebels now numbered almost 6,000. So Crixus, Castus and
Oenomaus went out to grab takeaway food for everyone.

AS IN TAKE
IT AWAY
FROM THE
ROMANS...

In the days before the former slaves had defeated
Glaber, they had lived off what they could take from

isolated villas and farms around Vesuvius. Now there were several thousand of them, they could take on bigger targets...

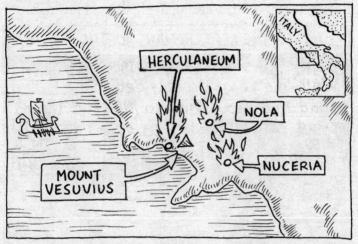

Crixus and his friends attacked several of the big towns of Campania. Rich Romans awoke in their townhouses to find slaves on the rampage. Those that were lucky got away with their lives. Those that weren't (lucky that is) lived just long enough to see their towns burnt and ransacked. Spartacus tried to stop the wholesale slaughter of the Roman citizens but Crixus didn't listen.

Crixus thought that as long as he supplied the runaway slaves with food and recruits it didn't matter what he did to the Romans inside the towns. Besides, Crixus was hungry for more than just food. He wanted revenge...

Plenty of the slaves who joined the rebellion agreed with Crixus. After living life under the Roman whip these slaves wanted to make the Romans pay. And Crixus was the man to lead them. Not only that, but the raids on the Campanian towns meant that the slaves at Vesuvius were well supplied again. Tonnes of grain, wheat, olives, fruit, wine and cheese were carried off to feed the slaves. Occasionally Crixus sent the newly freed slaves back to the camp with the food and loot.

Soon Spartacus felt he had enough food and enough slaves to face any new Roman soldiers. Sending word to Crixus to meet him back at the camp, Spartacus began packing up Glaber's tents and equipment. Once Crixus arrived, Spartacus led his followers (now almost 10,000 strong) into the open countryside. They headed south, away from Rome. They weren't yet strong enough to take a city that big.

Furius's forces

Meanwhile Varinius had arrived in Campania from Rome. He had split his forces between himself and his two commanders, Furius (yes, that really was his name) and Cossinius. Let's meet the three thugs who were tracking Spartacus:

VARINIUS

LIKES: FIGHTING ON HORSEBACK AND GLORY.

DISLIKES: ANYONE WHO STANDS IN THE WAY OF HIS PROMOTION TO A HIGHER RANK.

NICKNAME: 'HORSEWHIP'.

CHARACTER: VERY CAUTIOUS, LIKES TO PLAY THINGS BY THE BOOK.

COSSINIUS

LIKES: BATHS.

DISLIKES: FIGHTING (TOO DIRTY).

NICKNAME: 'COSSINIUS THE CLEAN'.

CHARACTER: PREFERS SOAP AND SUDS TO SWORDS AND SLAUGHTER.

FURIUS

LIKES:	FIGHTING.
DISLIKES:	VARINIUS (TOO CAUTIOUS) AND COSSINIUS (TOO CLEAN).
NICKNAME:	DOESN'T NEED ONE; HIS NAME SAYS IT ALL.
CHARACTER:	THE YOUNGEST OF THE THREE WITH THE MOST TO PROVE.

Varinius didn't want to be caught out like Glaber. His plan was to get Furius to track the slaves without fighting them. Furius would keep Varinius informed of Spartacus's movements. Then Varinius would decide when and where to attack the slaves.

Furius had no problem tracking the slaves as they marched out from Vesuvius. What he did have a problem with was not being able to fight them. Furius had 2,000 men under his command. They might not have been the best troops ever (again, Rome hadn't sent its best legions out after Spartacus) but Furius still fancied his chances. After all the enemies weren't *proper* soldiers, they were mere slaves.

Setting the trap

Spartacus was thinking pretty much the same thing as Furius. The slaves weren't yet a fully trained army. Although they now had quite a few proper weapons (Glaber had really been very, very generous) they still weren't fully armed. And, between them, the three Roman thugs had six or seven thousand soldiers.

78

This is one of those times when the Roman writers came over all embarrassed about their own history, but we can guess at what happened next.

Spartacus probably realized that the young Roman desperately wanted to beat the slaves before Cossinius and Varinius got involved. As he and his followers marched he hatched a cunning plan…

I. Crixus to take 100 men to the back of our marching column and guard all the slaves that are only able to move slowly, like the old and the sick.

II. Guards and slow-movers to lag as far back as possible while we all march off. Furius will think he can easily take them out.

III. When Furius appears, Crixus and his band of men to wait on standby for further orders.

Sure enough, Crixus soon saw a plume of dust behind his little band of marchers. He led them into a small gully and waited.

Spartacus's trap was set…

Furius falls for it

Furius saw his chance. His troops lined up next to the gully, blocking the only way out. He had the slaves trapped! Visions of victory swam through the Roman's head…

The Legion
FIREBRAND
FURIUS
FLAILS
FUGITIVES!

Furius urged his troops forward. But as they advanced he noticed something odd. The slaves behind Crixus were disappearing. The gully had another way out! Furius was furious. He ordered his men to hurry up before all the slaves escaped. The Romans advanced toward Crixus, who stood his ground in the gully with his men. The Romans paused. Crixus only had 100 armed men; the Romans numbered almost 2,000. Why was Crixus so confident?

Suddenly Furius knew the reason. As soon as the Romans entered the gully they heard the sound of swords being drawn. Thousands of them. While Furius had been following Crixus he'd failed to notice the rest of the slave army had doubled back. Now the Romans were the ones trapped in the gully, surrounded by slaves.

Suddenly Furius didn't feel quite so heroic...

The Legion

FORUM FURY AS FORLORN FURIUS FAILS!

The battle of the bath

One thug down, two more to go!

Spartacus realized that after Furius's failure Varinius was likely to try and unite his two remaining armies. He knew that his best bet was to take on Cossinius and Varinius separately. So Spartacus divided his followers again. Most of them headed south. This time it was Spartacus who led a smaller gang of ex-slaves to hunt Romans, wherever they might be...

Spartacus had sent out spies and trackers to keep tabs on all the Roman generals. They were ordered to follow the Roman columns as they marched through Campania. They told Spartacus that Cossinius was 'taking a break' there from hunting slaves.

The Roman commander had followed Varinius's orders and had pitched his camp to block Spartacus marching north. But Cossinius quickly tired of living among his dirty troops. Frankly, he saw the whole slave hunt as an opportunity to visit the world-famous baths of Campania. So he decided to take a small force with him to visit the baths at a nearby villa. Unfortunately for them, someone else had the same idea…

Trying to run from a band of bloodthirsty slaves with only a towel and some soap is pretty difficult, but somehow Cossinius managed it. Spartacus pursued the general all the way to his camp. Once there, Spartacus and his followers managed to take the camp, slaughter the soldiers and kill Cossinius.

Once again Spartacus had shown that bravery, cunning and surprise could defeat the Romans.

Horsing around

Only Varinius was left now. His two commanders had been defeated. One was dead (but at least he was clean when he died) and his 6,000 soldiers had been reduced to around 2,000. Things looked unpleasant for the Roman official, but Varinius knew that to return to Rome having been beaten by a slave was not an option. (He'd never be promoted if he lost like Glaber.)

Varinius set up camp close to Spartacus. That way he hoped to keep an eye on the runaway slaves while staying well defended. Unfortunately (for the Roman), Spartacus had yet another cunning plan up his sleeve...

Spartacus fooled Varinius into thinking the camp was still occupied while he and his followers stole away from the Romans in the middle of the night. So Varinius had to leave his secure camp and follow Spartacus into the open countryside. He hoped to stop Spartacus marching north towards Rome.

But Spartacus had no intention of marching north. Instead, he rallied his men and, in a quick series of battles, defeated Varinius. The vanquished Varinius only narrowly escaped being taken prisoner by the slaves. In fact, Spartacus captured the Roman's beautiful white horse from under him. That wasn't all – Spartacus captured several Lictors (the men that carried the Fasces in front of the Roman armies) and another Fasces to add to his collection…

83

Southern Italy, 73 BC

It's got to be said, things are going rather well. The other night I was polishing my new fasces when the wife suddenly told me I am fast becoming a legend. It's quite a surprise when she says something that nice so I asked her what she meant. Of course she then said something about how I was probably going to come to a sticky end... Typical, she can't just say I'm a legend and leave it at that. Anyway, I told her I wouldn't be a proper legend until I've led all the slaves to freedom. To do that I'm going to need a proper army. First we need a proper name – I know, I'll call it the 'Army of Freed Slaves Who Want to Go Home'. Hmm, perhaps the 'Free Slave Army' has more of a ring to it.

Creating a proper army isn't something you can do overnight. It'll take time to recruit, equip and train former slaves to make them good soldiers. Mind you, if there's one thing all of us ex-gladiators know about it's training killers... Sounds like a plan to me!

NO GOLD, JUST IRON

With winter closing in Spartacus had plenty of time to think about what he'd need for his new army. They had defeated all of the soldiers Rome was going to send that year. Spartacus knew there would now be a break for winter. The Romans would keep their best troops in Rome (just in case) and wouldn't send anyone after the slaves until the spring. If they did send anyone out during the winter, they would suffer terrible losses from disease and lack of food.

So Spartacus had time to train his army. But what about recruiting more soldiers? At this point Spartacus and the gladiators commanded a force of about 10,000. The slaves of Campania had flocked to join the Free Slave Army as well as local thieves and bandits. But, in order to build an army that could beat the Roman legions, Spartacus needed thousands more to join. Each of Rome's legions was around 4,500 strong, but whenever they went to war they were joined by an equal number of foreign allies. So far Rome hadn't unleashed its full force. But if Spartacus continued to threaten their land and slaves, the senate was sure to act...

So where would Spartacus find the men, and the location, to build his army of freed slaves?

After the defeat of Varinius, Spartacus had the whole of southern Italy at his feet. The south was the poorest part of Italy. There were plenty of slaves and poor citizens. Nearby, there were two regions that Spartacus had his eyes on, Lucania and Apulia. Ideal places, in fact, for Spartacus to attract even more followers.

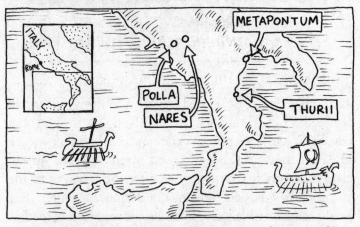

Of course the south was also quite a distance from Rome, so the slaves would have plenty of warning if a Roman army began marching after them. It was also warmer and it had beaches. At the very least the gladiators and slaves could enjoy a holiday before the fighting started again in the spring. So Spartacus and his followers turned south.

As the Free Slave Army marched, they displayed the captured emblems of the Roman armies they had defeated. The Fasces were held up by those marching in front. Spartacus himself rode on the beautiful white horse he had captured from underneath Varinius.

Each day members of the army went into the countryside. They found gangs of slaves chained together working the wheat fields. They found slaves working over hot furnaces in metal shops. Wherever they found these chained-up workers they urged them to join the uprising…

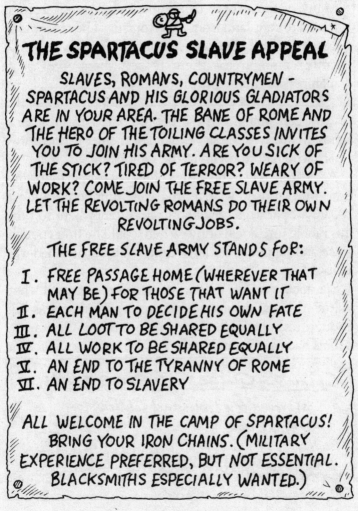

THE SPARTACUS SLAVE APPEAL

SLAVES, ROMANS, COUNTRYMEN – SPARTACUS AND HIS GLORIOUS GLADIATORS ARE IN YOUR AREA. THE BANE OF ROME AND THE HERO OF THE TOILING CLASSES INVITES YOU TO JOIN HIS ARMY. ARE YOU SICK OF THE STICK? TIRED OF TERROR? WEARY OF WORK? COME JOIN THE FREE SLAVE ARMY. LET THE REVOLTING ROMANS DO THEIR OWN REVOLTING JOBS.

THE FREE SLAVE ARMY STANDS FOR:

I. FREE PASSAGE HOME (WHEREVER THAT MAY BE) FOR THOSE THAT WANT IT
II. EACH MAN TO DECIDE HIS OWN FATE
III. ALL LOOT TO BE SHARED EQUALLY
IV. ALL WORK TO BE SHARED EQUALLY
V. AN END TO THE TYRANNY OF ROME
VI. AN END TO SLAVERY

ALL WELCOME IN THE CAMP OF SPARTACUS! BRING YOUR IRON CHAINS. (MILITARY EXPERIENCE PREFERRED, BUT NOT ESSENTIAL. BLACKSMITHS ESPECIALLY WANTED.)

Tens of thousands of slaves answered the call of Spartacus, as well as peasants who had been badly treated by the Romans.

When in Rome: Peasants
Many of the people of Apulia and Lucania were forced to rent land from rich Romans. The rent was very high and when they couldn't afford it, it was quite common for them to sell themselves or members of their family into slavery.

As you can imagine these people hated the Romans almost as much as the slaves did. For them, Spartacus was a hero who had stood up to the tyrants.

As Spartacus marched, the column of people following him grew and grew. Eventually it numbered almost 100,000. Spartacus now had to find somewhere to turn this rabble into a real army. Where could he find enough space and supplies for a large camp? What he needed was a city.

Spartacus and his fellow commanders discussed what tactics they could use to capture a city that was big enough to cope with their huge number. Of course, Crixus had his own methods:

Crixus's Guide to Taking a City
I. March a few thousand soldiers to the front gate

II. Knock on the door and ask to be let in

"Let us in"

III. If they let you in, immediately start looting and burning

IV. If they don't let you in, appeal to the slaves inside to rebel

"rebel!"

V. Once inside immediately start looting and burning

VI. If still outside after steps I and IV immediately start looting and burning anyway

Spartacus wasn't happy with Crixus's tactics. He wanted to take a city intact. A burnt-out shell wasn't much use as a training camp. He told Crixus and the others that they were to try and negotiate with the city councils.

"SPOIL SPART!"

Unfortunately for the luckless cities of Lucania, Spartacus didn't convince Crixus. As they passed Nares and Polla, Spartacus tried to stop Crixus's followers from trashing the towns. He even went as far as sending a messenger to warn local townsfolk that Crixus was coming. But the messages arrived too late. Crixus was bent on revenge.

> If Crixus doesn't stop burning all these cities to the ground, we'll never find anywhere to train the army. He's beginning to really get on my wick. I don't even need the wife to tell me... If we don't find somewhere soon, Crixus and I are going to have a blazing row.

The Gauls who followed Crixus fell in with all the bandits and thieves who had joined the Free Slave Army in Campania. They didn't care about going home and they didn't care about putting an end to slavery. They cared about gold and silver, horses and wine. And getting sweet revenge against the Romans.

While the army had been small this hadn't been a problem. But now Crixus's followers were causing mayhem. They refused to follow orders and were preventing the rest of the army from finding a training camp. As they approached the southern coast of Italy the rows between Spartacus and Crixus got worse. Spartacus was desperate to make peace with the people of Thurii so that the army could camp nearby and use the city. He was afraid that Crixus would sack the town, as he had at Nares and Polla. This time Spartacus made sure he went to see the town council himself.

The town council of Thurii accepted Spartacus's promise that the slaves would not burn the city down. It's possible Spartacus's charm won them over, but the chest full of jewels and gold he gave them as a down payment on food and supplies probably helped (along with the 80,000 soldiers he had with him). They set aside a big patch of land on the coast for the Free Slave Army to use as its winter quarters.

Camp 'Free Slave Army'

You may have been to a campsite on your holidays but you've never been to anything like the one Spartacus had to run during the winter of 73–72 BC. With more than 80,000 people needing shelter, food and training, Spartacus was a very busy man...

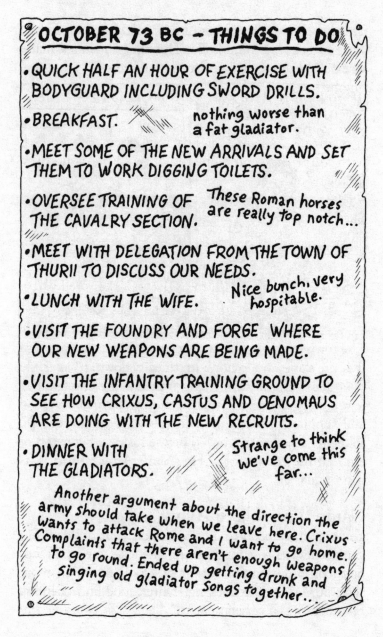

OCTOBER 73 BC – THINGS TO DO

- QUICK HALF AN HOUR OF EXERCISE WITH BODYGUARD INCLUDING SWORD DRILLS.

- BREAKFAST. *nothing worse than a fat gladiator.*

- MEET SOME OF THE NEW ARRIVALS AND SET THEM TO WORK DIGGING TOILETS.

- OVERSEE TRAINING OF THE CAVALRY SECTION. *These Roman horses are really top notch...*

- MEET WITH DELEGATION FROM THE TOWN OF THURII TO DISCUSS OUR NEEDS.

- LUNCH WITH THE WIFE. *Nice bunch, very hospitable.*

- VISIT THE FOUNDRY AND FORGE WHERE OUR NEW WEAPONS ARE BEING MADE.

- VISIT THE INFANTRY TRAINING GROUND TO SEE HOW CRIXUS, CASTUS AND OENOMAUS ARE DOING WITH THE NEW RECRUITS.

- DINNER WITH THE GLADIATORS. *Strange to think we've come this far...*

Another argument about the direction the army should take when we leave here. Crixus wants to attack Rome and I want to go home. Complaints that there aren't enough weapons to go round. Ended up getting drunk and singing old gladiator songs together..

These weren't the only arguments that Spartacus had with his gladiator friends. It's easy to divide loot equally when there are a few hundred people, but with an army numbering almost 100,000 it's a lot harder. Arguments about how it was distributed were becoming more and more frequent.

Spartacus thought long and hard about how to deal with all of these problems. Eventually he issued the following order:

GENERAL ORDER No. 1 FOR THE FREE SLAVE ARMY BY ORDER OF SPARTACUS, THE GLADIATOR GENERAL

- NO EX-SLAVE IS TO BRING, BY TRADE OR LOOTING, GOLD INTO THE SLAVE CAMP AT THURII.
- ANY GOLD FOUND (OR STOLEN) IS TO BE COLLECTED AND TRADED IN LOCAL MARKETS FOR IRON AND FOOD.
- HOARD IRON IN VAST QUANTITIES – ANY OLD CHAINS AND MANACLES TO BE HANDED TO THE CAMP BLACKSMITHS.

WARNING!
ANYONE FOUND WITH GOLD WILL BE KICKED OUT OF THE ARMY.

Spartacus knew the army needed metal it could turn into weapons and armour. Gold might look nice, but it was too soft to make into swords or shields. Besides, the rows over the loot were beginning to disrupt the training. But

93

for Crixus and his followers this order was the final straw. They'd put up with Spartacus being elected leader over Crixus. They'd put up with his talk of returning all the slaves to their homes. They'd even put up with his insistence that all the loot should be shared equally. Now that Spartacus was banning gold from the camp they were deeply unhappy.

Thurii, 73 BC

Crixus is furious. He's rounding up all his followers - there's between 20,000 and 30,000 of them! They want to take the weapons (Crixus says it was his gold that paid for them) and form their own camp. Well he's not taking the equipment. That loot was shared out equally and my new Free Slave Army is going to need those weapons to fight its way home. Hopefully Crixus will cool down - if he doesn't we'll have to settle this, **gladiator style!** He knows I'm just as capable of playing the hard-man as he is.

Spartacus   Crixus

It can't come to this, can it?

Luckily it didn't come to an all-out fight. In the end Crixus and Spartacus reached a deal. Crixus would establish a smaller camp near the main Free Slave Army. He would continue to train his troops along with Spartacus until the spring.

All winter more slaves had arrived from the surrounding countryside so the loss of Crixus's men was not that serious for Spartacus. But it didn't stop Spartacus feeling upset that his old friend was going to leave...

Thurii, 72 BC

Crixus left for his own camp today. Last night, we had a drink together and remembered the old times – fighting in the arena together, breaking out of Batiatus's school and beating all those Romans. Just as he left he gave me a final bit of advice: 'Even if you make it all the way north, the army will never cross the Alps, Spartacus. We slaves can never go home. You'll have to free all the slaves of Italy and destroy Rome before we can be truly free.' (I wonder if he's been talking to the wife?) I told him I didn't care, I'm still going to try and get the slaves home. He said, 'I'd rather live a year as a rich rogue than spend my time dreaming dreams of something that might not happen.' Then he left. Of course I'll see him again soon (he's only moving to the next valley over) but when the weather gets better we'll be going our separate ways.

The wife says Crixus is being silly. She said something about him being brought low by the letter 'G'. I certainly hope Crixus gets on OK, but we're better off without him. If we had to stop the march every time he wanted to loot a village we'd never get to the Alps. I was elected to get these slaves home, and by the chains I used to wear, that's what I intend to do.

Far to the north, at the other end of the country, lay a massive mountain range that separated Italy from the rest of Europe. The Alps formed a natural barrier between Rome and the parts of Europe they plundered to get their slaves. Once across the mountains, Spartacus planned to disband the army and send everyone home. Of course, 'home' was a different place for everyone, but Spartacus was sure that once they were free from the Romans they'd all find their way back to their homelands.

A few weeks after Crixus moved away from the Free Slave Army, Spartacus received the news everyone had been waiting for. A delegation of village elders from Thurii came to see him. They had some information from Rome...

The Legion

~ February 72 BC ~

SENATE TAKES SLAVES SERIOUSLY

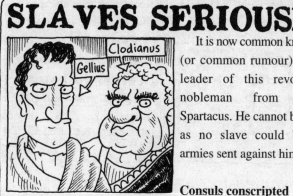

Clodianus

Gellius

It is now common knowledge (or common rumour) that the leader of this revolt is a nobleman from Thrace, Spartacus. He cannot be a slave as no slave could beat the armies sent against him.

Two new consuls have been appointed for the New Year. They are Gnaeus Cornelius Lentulus Clodianus, and Lucius Gellius Publicola.

Consuls consulted

The senate asked the new consuls how they would handle the uprising of slaves currently plaguing southern Italy. Both said they now considered the situation 'beyond a joke'. 'The best way to crush a slave revolt is to crush it with military might,' said Clodianus.

Consuls conscripted

The consuls have been asked to deal with the uprising immediately. This time, however, Rome will send proper armies. Four legions of over 4,000 soldiers each will accompany the consuls on their way into battle. A similar number of Rome's allies will also be going along for the fight.

Consuls coming

Having placed the two consuls at the head of a full army, Rome has sent a clear message to the slaves and anyone found

97

helping them. WATCH IT! This time there will be no mistakes. When asked if he had a personal message for the gladiator general, Gellius remarked, '*Age, Spartacus. Fac ut gaudeam.*'*

*Go ahead, Spartacus. Make my day!

How Rome works
Consuls: Two new consuls are appointed each year in Rome. They look after the republic's warfare and welfare. They lead armies, enforce laws and keep the slaves (and foreigners) in check. These guys are the top dogs.

The local councillors of Thurii wanted Spartacus to move fast. They didn't want the Romans to catch up with him anywhere near their town. The Romans would be angry enough that the people of Thurii helped the slaves, and they'd certainly want to raid the town's grain stores for food. But, since the slaves had been around there wasn't much grain left. So the council asked if Spartacus wouldn't mind awfully going and fighting the Romans somewhere else.

Spartacus understood why they wanted him to go, but he had already decided the time had come for the Free Slave Army to move on – and fast. If the Romans marched quickly enough they would block the route north and the Free Slave Army would be caught with its back to the sea. Having sent a message to Crixus, Spartacus started to get the Free Slave Army ready to march north to the Alps.

TWO CONSULS, FOUR LEGIONS AND A FUNERAL

What a difference a few months can make!

When Spartacus arrived in Thurii he had around 100,000 followers. They were poorly equipped, poorly fed, poorly trained and, well, just poor really. Even after the split with Crixus, Spartacus's Free Slave Army numbered around 70,000. (That's 1,000 times the number of gladiators that escaped Batiatus's school!)

Spartacus had spent time in the Roman army and had seen it fighting from both sides. He had used all his experience to build a disciplined and well-equipped army. Most of the troops had proper weapons. They had iron swords with iron or bronze armour and shields. They were organized into disciplined units. Those long, hard days at the gladiator school had left their mark. (Literally, as the gladiators still had the name 'Batiatus' burned into their legs.) The Free Slave Army had been trained by gladiators to fight like gladiators. They had practised with their swords and spears over and over again. The gladiators had taught them how to find glory in battle, treat death with contempt and, most importantly, how to kill. They knew that defeat meant death and victory probably just meant another fight was around the corner. But they were ready.

After packing away their camp, the Free Slave Army got into their marching formation. Each unit gathered

THE FREE SLAVE ARMY ORDER OF BATTLE

I. THE GRUESOME GAULS MADE UP OF THE GAULS WHO HAVEN'T FOLLOWED CRIXUS. INCLUDES THE MOST EXPERIENCED VETERANS OF THE SLAVE ARMY.

II. THE THRACIAN GUARD SPARTACUS'S PERSONAL GUARD. ARMED WITH THE BEST THRACIAN-STYLE WEAPONS AND PERSONALLY SELECTED AND TRAINED BY THE GREAT MAN HIMSELF. ALSO FUNCTIONS AS AN INFANTRY UNIT.

III. THE FIGHTING ITALIANS HEAVILY ARMOURED. MADE UP OF POOR ROMAN CITIZENS AND SLAVES FROM ALL OVER THE KNOWN WORLD. MOST SEEKING REVENGE AGAINST ROME.

WE GOTTA LOTTA GAUL

HOME OR ROME!

NO JUSTICE, NO PEACE

COMMANDER IN CHIEF: SPARTACUS

SUB-COMMANDERS: OENOMAUS, CASTUS, GANNICUS

behind its own military standard. This would help them identify one another and also tell them where to go during a battle. On each standard there were also scenes from the former slaves' homelands. It helped them remember why they were about to march against the Roman legions.

101

Finally the Free Slave Army began the long march north. As they streamed out of the camp near Thurii the townspeople watched them go. (They were probably just making sure that Spartacus had actually left.)

Thurii, 72 BC

It's incredible! A few years ago I was shepherding a bunch of woolly sheep around on the edge of a forest in Thrace. Now I'm leading a huge army slap-bang in the middle of Italy. How times change. Still, there's a lot to be said for a nice quiet life back in the old Thracian village:

1. No more arguing ex-slaves.
2. No more gladiator contests.
3. No more Romans trying to kill me. (I hope.)

Never mind, I've got it all planned out, we march north, avoid the city of Rome, cross the Alps, and go home. It's a simple plan so I'm sure it'll work. I've prepared the army's marching orders:

- Keep in your units
- Obey those more senior and experienced than you

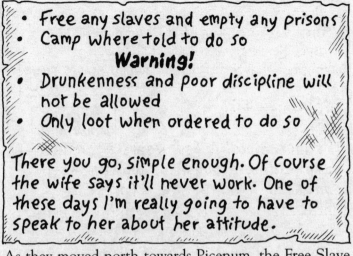

- Free any slaves and empty any prisons
- Camp where told to do so
  ### Warning!
- Drunkenness and poor discipline will not be allowed
- Only loot when ordered to do so

There you go, simple enough. Of course the wife says it'll never work. One of these days I'm really going to have to speak to her about her attitude.

As they moved north towards Picenum, the Free Slave Army freed slaves wherever they found them. The events of the last year had meant that the Romans had been getting even tougher with their slaves. Their harsh punishments got harsher. Many slaves were locked up in prisons but thousands managed to escape or were freed by Spartacus and joined the Free Slave Army.

Crixus and his 30,000 followers had left Thurii a few hours after Spartacus, but unlike the Free Slave Army their goal wasn't freeing more slaves. In fact, Crixus's route was rather different from that of Spartacus and the Free Slave Army:

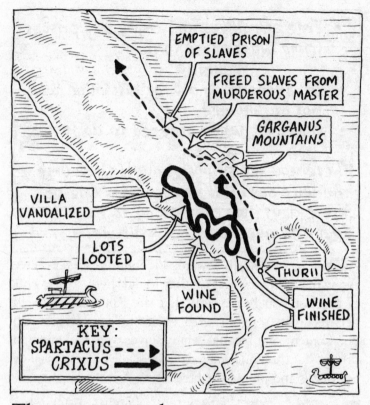

The canny consuls

Meanwhile, the two consuls had left Rome and were on their way to crush the slave rebellion.

Clodianus and Gellius were no fools. They weren't desperate to succeed like Furius. They could afford to wait. They knew that to take on Crixus's army as well as Spartacus's army would be foolish. Their plan depended on the Roman legions being able to pick off each army one at a time. That meant waiting until the gap between the two rebel slave armies was wide enough.

Soon the consuls saw their chance.

AS THE ROMANS BEGAN TO OVERWHELM HIS FORCES, CRIXUS SENT RUNNERS TO SPARTACUS.

TELL SPARTACUS WE MIGHT NEED A HAND OVER HERE...

MEANWHILE, HOWEVER, SPARTACUS HAD TROUBLE OF HIS OWN. CLODIANUS HAD DRAWN UP HIS LEGIONS IN A DOUBLE BATTLE LINE ACROSS A HILL IN FRONT OF THE FREE SLAVE ARMY. THE ARMY HAD TO MARCH THROUGH THEM TO CONTINUE NORTH. BUT THIS WAS WHY SPARTACUS HAD SPENT THE WINTER TRAINING HIS SOLDIERS. QUICKLY THEY FELL INTO FORMATION AND CHARGED!

THESE BATTLES CAN BE REALLY DANGEROUS THINGS.

CLODIANUS KNEW THAT WHILE SPARTACUS WAS FIGHTING IN PICENUM, GELLIUS WOULD BE FREE TO ATTACK CRIXUS, BUT WHILE HE WAS HAPPY TO WATCH HIS LEGIONARIES FEND OFF THE ATTACKING SLAVES FOR AS LONG AS THEY COULD, HIS SOLDIERS WEREN'T SO HAPPY. CLEARLY THE SLAVES WERE RATHER BETTER AT FIGHTING THAN THE ROMANS THOUGHT. FINALLY CLODIANUS PULLED HIS SOLDIERS AWAY FROM THE SLAUGHTER.

RUN! THAT'S JUST WHAT I WAS ABOUT TO SAY!

It was a vital victory for the slaves. They'd smashed two Roman legions and forced a mighty consul to flee. With Clodianus out of the way, the Alps were one step closer. But Spartacus and his army didn't have time to celebrate. Crixus's runners had arrived with news of the Garganus incident.

GATHER THE GLADIATORS, WE'VE GOT TO GET TO GARGANUS!

As they marched south, they met Arrius and Gellius coming the other way. The two Romans had thought they'd creep up behind Spartacus while he fought Clodianus. Instead they met the Free Slave Army head on. Needless to say Spartacus was in no mood for a long fight. Already weakened by Crixus's heroic stand, Arrius and Gellius were soon sent packing.

But it was a bitter victory for the Free Slave Army. Spartacus arrived at Garganus too late...

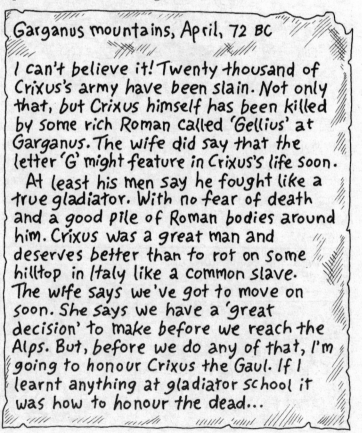

Garganus mountains, April, 72 BC

I can't believe it! Twenty thousand of Crixus's army have been slain. Not only that, but Crixus himself has been killed by some rich Roman called 'Gellius' at Garganus. The wife did say that the letter 'G' might feature in Crixus's life soon.

At least his men say he fought like a true gladiator. With no fear of death and a good pile of Roman bodies around him. Crixus was a great man and deserves better than to rot on some hilltop in Italy like a common slave. The wife says we've got to move on soon. She says we have a 'great decision' to make before we reach the Alps. But, before we do any of that, I'm going to honour Crixus the Gaul. If I learnt anything at gladiator school it was how to honour the dead...

Spartacus set up camp in the Garganus mountains. He carefully placed guards around its perimeter (as Crixus should have done) and sent out scouts to report on Gellius and Clodianus.

After making sure that the consuls weren't planning any more nasty surprises for him, Spartacus set about honouring his dead friend.

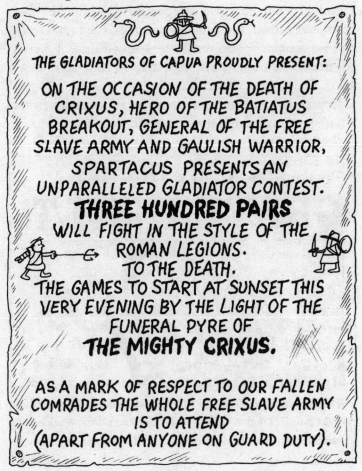

THE GLADIATORS OF CAPUA PROUDLY PRESENT:

ON THE OCCASION OF THE DEATH OF CRIXUS, HERO OF THE BATIATUS BREAKOUT, GENERAL OF THE FREE SLAVE ARMY AND GAULISH WARRIOR, SPARTACUS PRESENTS AN UNPARALLELED GLADIATOR CONTEST. **THREE HUNDRED PAIRS** WILL FIGHT IN THE STYLE OF THE ROMAN LEGIONS. TO THE DEATH. THE GAMES TO START AT SUNSET THIS VERY EVENING BY THE LIGHT OF THE FUNERAL PYRE OF **THE MIGHTY CRIXUS.**

AS A MARK OF RESPECT TO OUR FALLEN COMRADES THE WHOLE FREE SLAVE ARMY IS TO ATTEND (APART FROM ANYONE ON GUARD DUTY).

You might ask where Spartacus was going to find 600 people to fight in honour of his friend. Well, true to form most of the Romans had either run away or been killed after the battles with Clodianus and Gellius. But around 600 of them had been taken prisoner. They must have been puzzled when the slaves gave each of them a sword and a shield. Perhaps they thought they were about to be recruited by Spartacus. Perhaps they thought they were going to be freed. But they soon learned the brutal truth.

The Roman prisoners were forced into a group together. On all sides the Free Slave Army surrounded them. Escape was impossible.

Spartacus stood and the crowd went quiet. Then the trumpets sounded and the command rang out:

'Let the games begin!'

The Daily Gladius
GRAVE INSULT!

Never has the honourable sport of gladiatorial combat been so shamed. Last night the rebel Thracian Spartacus thumbed his nose at Rome's fine tradition of public slaughter and butchery.

Arena authorities were helpless as the former gladiator forced 600 Romans to fight in front of an audience of slave scum. Fighting in pairs, the Romans killed one another in a desperate bid to survive. In a move calculated to insult the Roman people, Spartacus held these 'games' to 'honour' a fallen comrade. Crixus the Gaul was a despicable and insulting opponent of Rome. A petty bandit, Crixus deserved to be nailed to a cross not treated as a nobleman.

Panic!

This Spartacus character has got far too big for his boots. He has now defeated Rome's most senior politicians, leaving the city itself in the firing line of the slave rebellion. Treating Roman citizens as slaves by forcing them to fight to the death is the last straw.

The consuls know they are a laughing stock in the streets of Rome. Wisely they have decided not to return to Rome. Instead they have regrouped and will attempt to stop the slaves overrunning the city. On current form this newspaper thinks now is a good time to panic.

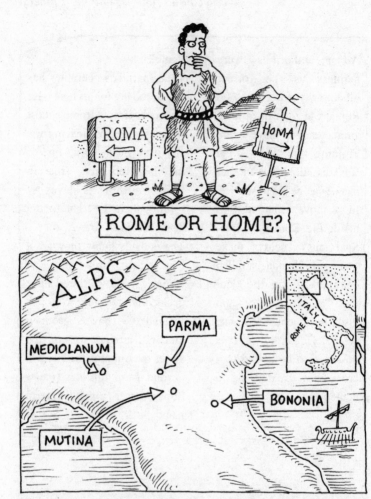

ROME OR HOME?

The citizens of Rome hadn't really taken Spartacus and the slave uprising seriously until now. They hadn't expected Spartacus and a few hundred escaped slaves to defeat the 3,000 men they'd sent against them. And they certainly hadn't expected Spartacus to survive the three-pronged attacks of Varinius, Cossinius and Furius. There had been large slave uprisings before, but never in

Italy itself and definitely not this close to Rome. On the streets of the capital, the citizens of Rome began to wonder if they were safe from this gladiator upstart, this Spartacus character.

When reports arrived that Spartacus had defeated what was left of the consuls' armies, the Romans waited for news of a Free Slave Army attack on the city. But Spartacus knew such an attack was out of the question...

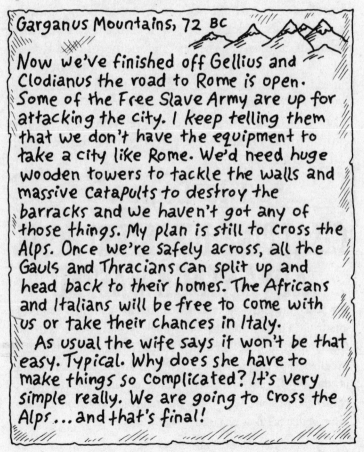

Garganus Mountains, 72 BC

Now we've finished off Gellius and Clodianus the road to Rome is open. Some of the Free Slave Army are up for attacking the city. I keep telling them that we don't have the equipment to take a city like Rome. We'd need huge wooden towers to tackle the walls and massive catapults to destroy the barracks and we haven't got any of those things. My plan is still to cross the Alps. Once we're safely across, all the Gauls and Thracians can split up and head back to their homes. The Africans and Italians will be free to come with us or take their chances in Italy.

As usual the wife says it won't be that easy. Typical. Why does she have to make things so complicated? It's very simple really. We are going to cross the Alps...and that's final!

The Free Slave Army marched north and soon reached the Roman province of Cisalpine Gaul. This was the last of Rome's northern Italian territories. They had arrived at the foothills of the Alps.

At Mutina (present-day Modena) the Free Slave Army ran into the Governor of Cisalpine Gaul, Gaius Cassius Longinus and a magistrate called Gnaeus Manlius. Longinus was an experienced Roman commander and the 10,000 men under his command were all hardened legionaries. They were used to fighting barbarian hordes. They were defending one of Rome's richest colonies. They were highly motivated and trained. Why should they worry about some marauding slaves to the south?

But Spartacus and the Free Slave Army were in fine fighting form. There was only ever going to be one result in the coming combat...

❧The Legion ❧

CISALPINE DISASTER! HOME ADVANTAGE WASTED

For years, the garrisons which guard the northern border of Cisalpine Gaul have done an excellent job defending our northern border against barbarian invasion.

But all that has now changed.

Spartacus and his band of runaway slaves attacked the Roman positions from behind – only a lowly gladiator would think of such a tactic. He's certainly no nobleman. It's just not war!

Runaway Romans
Cassius 'didn't last very'
Longinus and Gnaeus 'not very'

Manlius only managed to escape at the last minute. Abandoning their soldiers and Rome's richest region, the two generals fled. At least by running away they were following a fine tradition of Roman generals fighting Spartacus and his army.

And, like the other generals sent against the renegade slave, Longinus found his way back to Rome. There he made his 'report' to the senate and was quickly relieved of command.

The last obstacle to the journey home had been removed. The Free Slave Army paused for breath. After all, they had marched the length of Italy in just a few months – that's over 600 miles. The slaves who survived all the way from Capua and Vesuvius had marched half that again. The army had fought battles against some of Rome's best soldiers. Now there was no one left for them to fight.

Rome alone

It just so happened that Spartacus and his troops were in one of Rome's wealthiest provinces. Definitely the sort of place the tired army could enjoy a last bit of R'n'R (Revenge and Rowdiness) at the expense of the rich Romans.

But while Spartacus and the Free Slave Army took advantage of the local countryside, Rome was in uproar. Despite the fact that Spartacus had continued north and showed no sign of attacking the city, the Romans were worried. Their best generals were away fighting in foreign lands. Pompey the Great was in Spain fighting Roman rebels and Lucius Licinius Lucullus was in Asia, fighting King Mithridates (again).

In the streets of Rome, panic was spreading. A restless mob, already angry at the poor distribution of wheat and corn and worried that the uprising might stop food getting to the capital at all, headed for the Forum demanding the senate deal with the Spartacus question.

Who would defend the city of Rome? they asked. Was there someone who could defeat the slave threat? There was only one Roman official for the job – only one who was man enough to take on Spartacus…

MARCUS LICINIUS CRASSUS

LIKES:	MONEY, PROPERTY, SLAVES AND MONEY
DISLIKES:	POOR PEOPLE, SLAVES, AND OTHER ROMAN GENERALS (ESPECIALLY POMPEY THE GREAT – TOO YOUNG AND SUCCESSFUL)
NICKNAME:	'CRASSUS THE CRUEL', 'MONEYBAGS', 'MISER'
CHARACTER:	A SHREWD BUSINESSMAN WITH AN EYE TO HOLDING HIGH PUBLIC OFFICE. MAKES HIS MONEY BY BUYING PROPERTY AT CUT-DOWN RATES (AS IN, ACCEPT THIS AMOUNT OR GET CUT DOWN). EMPLOYS THOUSANDS OF SLAVES TO DO UP THE PROPERTIES BEFORE SELLING THEM FOR A HUGE PROFIT.

Crassus once said, 'No man can be accounted rich that cannot maintain an army at his own cost and charges.' Well, the senate was about to ask him to prove it.

Of course, crafty Crassus wasn't about to spend his vast fortune defending Rome for nothing. He knew that if he successfully guarded his fellow citizens they'd be in his debt. Then he could call in the favour and convince them to appoint him consul, or, even better, dictator.

When in Rome: Dictators

Occasionally Rome faced a crisis that the senate, the consuls and the other magistrates just couldn't deal with. In these cases the consuls and the senate appointed a dictator. Usually a dictator only held office for six months. But occasionally a dictator could use his military muscle to stay in power for a lot longer than that...

For Crassus, being the richest, most powerful citizen of the richest and most powerful nation in the world was the ultimate ambition. If he failed, well, there wouldn't be much of Rome left to rule. So Crassus got on with the job of raising an army...

Mutiny at Mutina

Meanwhile, far to the north, the Free Slave Army was still enjoying Alpine hospitality...

117

Mutina, 72 BC

We've already stayed too long in this place. All the slaves are getting fat on this great food. Even the wife says it's really good. Of course, she's got something else to grumble about. She told me the other night that if we don't move soon we'll be in serious trouble. Apparently the Romans have appointed a new commander to take us on. To cap it all she says the Romans might recall Pompey and my old boss Triple 'L' himself. Even fully equipped we'd have trouble beating all three of them. I wish she didn't seem quite so happy to give me the bad news.

I told her it didn't matter because I'll be ordering the army across the Alps any day now. In a few weeks the weather will turn bad and the mountains will be impossible to cross. She laughed at that and said, 'But I haven't given you the really bad news yet, Spartacus. The army are on the verge of mutiny.'

We're so close to home, just one more push to get everyone across the mountains then the wife and I can retire. That was the plan, and it still is. Surely it can't go wrong now?

The plan might have been a simple one, but Spartacus was having trouble convincing the Free Slave Army that they should cross the Alps and head home.

The problem for Spartacus was that the Free Slave Army was no longer made up of ex-gladiators and foreign slaves. During the long march from the south Spartacus had attracted more and more poor Romans. Also many of the runaway slaves had been born into slavery. For these people, home wasn't across the Alps – it was right there in Italy. And that wasn't the only reason why the army was unwilling to follow Spartacus. Things had changed in the minds of the soldiers of the Free Slave Army. They were no longer downtrodden and beaten people. Suddenly they were thinking for themselves and questioning everyone in authority, including Spartacus.

Soon, even Spartacus was questioning his plan…

Mutina, 72 BC

The problem is I'm not sure I really want to go home now either; I was doing all of this for the freed slaves. I've led an army of 100,000, defeated the armies of Rome and picked up some really nice horses along the way. Do I really want to go back to tending a couple of sheep in Thrace? Not really.

Without an army I'm just a nobody, and without me the army will go and do something stupid like attack Rome. They will surely be defeated and then all my hard work will have been for nothing.

To cap it all whenever I ask the wife for advice she just smiles and talks about that snake in Rome. It's all giving me a headache.

Most of the Free Slave Army wanted to stay in Italy and there was nothing Spartacus could do about it.

So what was he to do?

Just as he had done at Vesuvius, Spartacus decided to call a mass meeting to come up with a plan everyone could agree with. These were the options the army came up with for discussion:

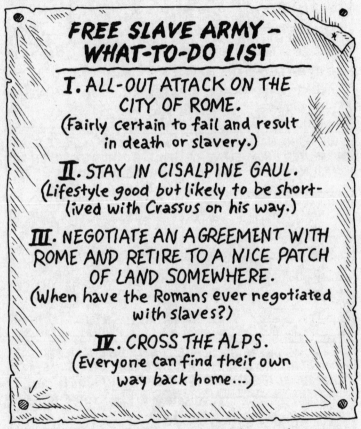

FREE SLAVE ARMY – WHAT-TO-DO LIST

I. ALL-OUT ATTACK ON THE CITY OF ROME.
(Fairly certain to fail and result in death or slavery.)

II. STAY IN CISALPINE GAUL.
(Lifestyle good but likely to be short-lived with Crassus on his way.)

III. NEGOTIATE AN AGREEMENT WITH ROME AND RETIRE TO A NICE PATCH OF LAND SOMEWHERE.
(When have the Romans ever negotiated with slaves?)

IV. CROSS THE ALPS.
(Everyone can find their own way back home...)

No one could agree on any of these ideas so the meeting dragged on and on. Finally, the army called on Spartacus to speak. The former shepherd boy from Thrace didn't disappoint. Spartacus had come up with yet another daring scheme.

121

By the end of the meeting the arguments about what they should do were raging even more fiercely than before. But most of the Free Slave Army wanted to stick with Spartacus. After all, he had led them to victory before. Here was a man they could trust. Eventually the whole Free Slave Army warmed to Spartacus's Sicily scheme. It was time to pack up the Alpine camp and head south.

LETHAL LOTTERIES AND MARINE MONSTERS

Sicily's huge Roman estates were packed with slaves. They were treated so badly that even some Romans had asked questions about their treatment. Of course, these Romans had only expressed an interest after some slaves had rebelled and killed their masters. Between 135 and 132 BC two slaves called Eunus and Kleon had rampaged around the island. They executed slave masters and caused general mayhem. Eunus actually went so far as declaring himself king. The Romans eventually crushed the revolt (and allowed Eunus to die, covered in lice, in prison).

WHAT A LOUSY WAY TO DIE!

Thirty years later another two troublemakers, Athenion and Salvius, did exactly the same thing. For a time it seemed they would be able to take over the island, but again the Romans were able to defeat them.

Spartacus would certainly have heard of these slave uprisings on Sicily. He probably also realized that if the first was in 135 BC and the second was in 104 BC then the next revolt should be scheduled for around now (72 BC). Spartacus might be a bit late but the slaves of Sicily wouldn't mind. They would remember how their ancestors had fought against the Romans and would join the Free Slave Army immediately. At least that was what Spartacus hoped would happen.

Fighting fit

With the Free Slave Army finally signed up to his plan, Spartacus began to think ahead. Freeing Sicily was not going to be easy. The first thing he needed to tackle was the general state of the army. Weapons had to be replaced and fixed. The fighting units had to be brought back to strength with new recruits. Soldiers who'd enjoyed too much food and wine had to be got back into shape.

While Spartacus was training the Free Slave Army, he sent out raiding parties to steal food from the local farmers. Sicily is over 600 miles away from Cisalpine

Gaul. To march the length of Italy (again) would require stocks of food. Local slaves who had run away from their masters helped by showing the raiders where the stores were kept. Then, the city prisons were emptied and the prisoners recruited to join Spartacus's army.

The next problem Spartacus faced was funds. The Free Slave Army would need all the money it could lay its hands on to buy enough weapons and equipment to take Sicily from the Romans.

Once again the Thracian had a plan…

GENERAL ORDER No. II
FOR THE FREE SLAVE ARMY
BY ORDER OF SPARTACUS,
THE GLADIATOR GENERAL

• ALL MEMBERS OF THE FREE SLAVE ARMY ARE TO COLLECT AS MUCH LOOT AS POSSIBLE. GOLD, GEMS OR VALUABLES ARE ALL ACCEPTABLE.

• ANY TREASURE FOUND (OR STOLEN) IS TO BE COLLECTED AND DEPOSITED IN THE FREE SLAVE ARMY'S NEW TREASURY.

WARNING!
ANYONE FOUND HOARDING GOLD FOR THEMSELVES WILL BE KICKED OUT OF THE ARMY.

Spartacus used some of the loot to buy more supplies. Money was exchanged for whatever weapons and equipment could be paid for. Anyone who didn't want to sell was quickly made an offer they couldn't refuse.

After a few weeks the Free Slave Army was ready. The units formed up for the long march back south and in the late summer of 72 BC it set out. Its new mission: 'Liberty or Death!'

Crossing Crassus

Meanwhile, Crassus was doing some preparation of his own. As well as taking over what was left of Clodianus's and Gellius's armies, Crassus had used his money and influence to recruit some of Rome's richest noblemen. They probably realized that after finishing off the slaves, Crassus would become even more important in Rome. But, of course, that had nothing to do with why they were fighting. Oh no, they just wanted to do their bit for Rome. If they happened to get rich and famous on the way, well, that would just be a bonus. Anyway, it wasn't the noblemen who were going to do the actual fighting. It was the poorer Roman citizens who would have to do the dirty work. Crassus had made sure he'd paid for enough of them as well.

All too soon, Spartacus's spies began to report back to their leader about Crassus's colossal army…

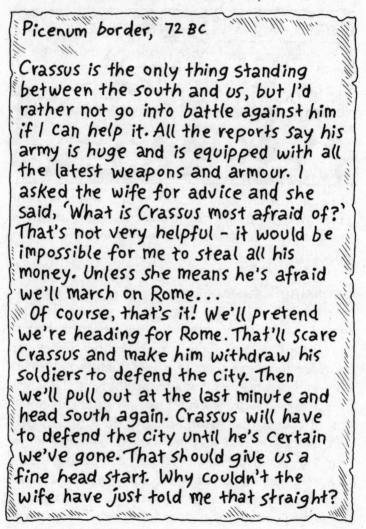

Picenum border, 72 BC

Crassus is the only thing standing between the south and us, but I'd rather not go into battle against him if I can help it. All the reports say his army is huge and is equipped with all the latest weapons and armour. I asked the wife for advice and she said, 'What is Crassus most afraid of?' That's not very helpful - it would be impossible for me to steal all his money. Unless she means he's afraid we'll march on Rome...

Of course, that's it! We'll pretend we're heading for Rome. That'll scare Crassus and make him withdraw his soldiers to defend the city. Then we'll pull out at the last minute and head south again. Crassus will have to defend the city until he's certain we've gone. That should give us a fine head start. Why couldn't the wife have just told me that straight?

Spartacus (like his wife) was absolutely right. Crassus was much more concerned with defending Rome than with fighting the Free Slave Army. He had his army dig great defensive ditches around the city. If the Thracian wanted to march on Rome then Crassus was going to make things as hard as possible for him.

But Spartacus had no intention of marching into Rome. At the last minute the Free Slave Army turned away from the city. Instead, Spartacus led it into Picenum on Italy's eastern coast. If Crassus wanted to take on the slaves then he could do it in open countryside.

But Crassus wasn't ready to abandon his defences.

Instead, he sent out one of his commanders with two legions to follow Spartacus and see what he was up to. The commander in charge of this mission, who had the unfortunate name of Mummius, was under strict instructions…

Bet you can't guess what happened next…

❧ The Legion ❧

SPARTACUS STRIKES AGAIN!

Hopes of an early victory for Crassus against the renegade slaves were dashed yesterday. Despite sending a highly paid contingent of Rome's nobility after Spartacus, Crassus lost the opening battle of this new campaign. This was mainly due to the uselessness of one of his commanders, Mummius.

Thoroughly thrashed

At first Mummius followed his orders. His two legions circled the Thracian's forces. Moving up behind the slaves Mummius observed their movements and realized they were not heading for Rome. Instead they were marching away from the capital.

'I thought that was a sign of weakness,' said the young Roman, lamely.

Despite his orders Mummius rushed into battle. He clearly thought that the superior equipment of his new legions would deal a crushing blow to the rebel slaves. But within hours Mummius's men had been thoroughly thrashed. Whole divisions died while hundreds hastily hotfooted it away. Those that ran (including Mummy's boy Mummius), quickly stripped themselves of their heavy (and very expensive) armour and weapons so they could run more quickly.

Such shameful scenes have not been seen since Spartacus last put the Roman legions to flight.

'I want my Mummius' says Crassus

On hearing the disastrous news from the front Crassus called for Mummius to report to him. According to well-placed sources, Crassus gave the cowardly commander a 'rough going-over'. But, speaking to our reporter, Crassus dismissed the loss of so many men and equipment.

'I said my money could buy an army, I didn't say it would be a good one. They won't be disobeying orders again, I can assure you.'

Crassus was furious. His orders had been disobeyed, his men had been killed and lots of nice shiny new equipment had been lost. The Roman general had to act quickly or his army would fall apart. He decided to use one of the Roman army's most gruesome punishments: decimation. His soldiers had been afraid of Spartacus on the battlefield. So now Crassus decided to make them even more afraid of Crassus! Even Roman writers describe what follows as 'shameful' and 'terrible':

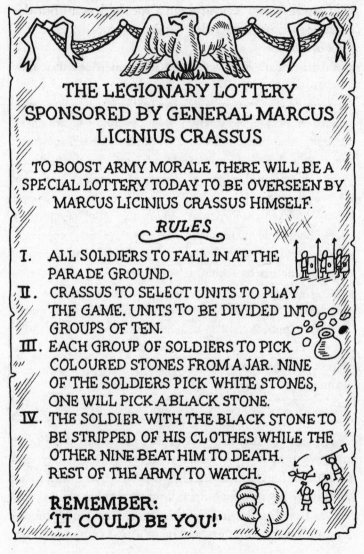

THE LEGIONARY LOTTERY
SPONSORED BY GENERAL MARCUS LICINIUS CRASSUS

TO BOOST ARMY MORALE THERE WILL BE A SPECIAL LOTTERY TODAY TO BE OVERSEEN BY MARCUS LICINIUS CRASSUS HIMSELF.

RULES

I.   ALL SOLDIERS TO FALL IN AT THE PARADE GROUND.

II. CRASSUS TO SELECT UNITS TO PLAY THE GAME. UNITS TO BE DIVIDED INTO GROUPS OF TEN.

III. EACH GROUP OF SOLDIERS TO PICK COLOURED STONES FROM A JAR. NINE OF THE SOLDIERS PICK WHITE STONES, ONE WILL PICK A BLACK STONE.

IV. THE SOLDIER WITH THE BLACK STONE TO BE STRIPPED OF HIS CLOTHES WHILE THE OTHER NINE BEAT HIM TO DEATH. REST OF THE ARMY TO WATCH.

REMEMBER:
'IT COULD BE YOU!'

Crassus chose the leftover legionaries from the armies of Mummius, Gellius and Clodianus to play the game. These were all soldiers that Spartacus had put to flight and Crassus was teaching them a special lesson. But the soldiers watching were also learning something – don't cross Crassus!

With his army now fully focused on the job in hand, Crassus led his troops south, after the Free Slave Army.

The secret mission

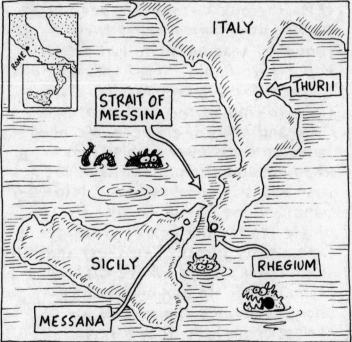

With the Romans out of the way Spartacus could start thinking about what he would need to do next. As the Free Slave Army marched along, raiding parties had been

Spartacus and his Glorious Gladiators

gathering money and precious metals for Spartacus's treasury. He'd used some of the money to buy new weapons, equipment and food, but was carefully putting together a secret stash. When he thought he had enough he sent for his two most trusted lieutenants…

Southern Italy, 72 BC

Last night I got Gannicus and Castus to come over to my tent. I showed them the box of loot I've been putting together. At first they thought I was about to run off with it but then I told them I was giving it to them for a secret mission. I want them to find us the best pirates in Italy and bring them here. We need boats to cross over to Sicily from Rhegium and the pirates have the best boats in the business. I told Gannicus and Castus to give the pirate leader the box of treasure (apparently pirates like that) and tell them there's more where that came from. That little box of treasure should convince the pirates we're serious. Hopefully they'll send someone along to negotiate with us when we reach Rhegium.

Without Gannicus and Castus Spartacus kept the Free Slave Army marching south. They were getting close to their destination: Rhegium and then – across the Strait of Messina – Sicily.

Spartacus had the Free Slave Army camp near Rhegium and patiently waited for his trusted lieutenants. To pass the time he held training exercises for the army, teaching swimming (in the sheltered coves near Rhegium) and invasion tactics. But each day he kept a look out for Gannicus and Castus and the pirates. Without ships the Free Slave Army would be stuck. Even with ships Spartacus was facing an even tougher challenge than the Roman legions…

Rhegium, 72 BC

The wife has been telling me the story of Odysseus and the Strait of Messina. Apparently the greatest Greek hero of them all was trying to sail through the strait but came up against two monsters, Charybdis and Scylla. Charybdis is a huge whirlpool that sucks ships to the very bottom of the ocean and drowns all the sailors. Then it spits them all out along the coast of Sicily. Scylla is a monster with six heads. Each head is like a dog's head but has three rows of teeth and is attached to a long neck. Apparently Scylla lives in the cliff faces on the Italian side and plucks sailors

from their ships and eats them. GRRR!
My wife really knows how to
make a man feel confident.
Of course I don't believe in these
monsters (although I had a bit of
trouble sleeping last night). I'm just
waiting for Gannicus and Castus to return.
If we're going to invade Sicily we need
ships to take us across. (And if we're
going to make it we'll need some sailors
who know how to avoid Scylla and
Charybdis!)

Spartacus's wife was right about the Strait of Messina – well, sort of. There weren't any monsters there but then there didn't really need to be. Although the Strait is only about 20 miles long and varies between two and ten miles wide, it is a truly terrifying stretch of water.

The pirate deal

The summer of 72 BC was almost over by the time Gannicus and Castus finally arrived in Rhegium, having completed their mission. Travelling with them to meet Spartacus was a delegation of pirates. It's possible that it even included the pirate king, Heracleo (a name feared by Romans almost as much as the name 'Spartacus').

Spartacus got down to business straight away. The Free Slave Army needed ships and it needed them now! News from the north was not good. Crassus had abandoned his huge defensive earthworks and was heading south. If the invasion of Sicily was to work (without Crassus harassing the army from behind) it would need to be done soon.

The pirates knew that Spartacus was desperate. They also knew that there was no way across to Sicily without lots of proper ships. At first they said they wouldn't be able take the whole of the army across. Then they said it would take them time to get the ships together.

THAT'S A LOT OF SHIPS YOU'RE TALKING ABOUT, GUV! COULD BE A BIT TRICKY... HOW ABOUT NEXT YEAR?

Spartacus pleaded with them. First he appealed to their common purpose, the Romans disliked pirates almost as much as they hated the slaves. When that didn't work he reminded the pirates that there would be lots of loot in it for them. Funnily enough, that did the trick. Finally a deal was struck.

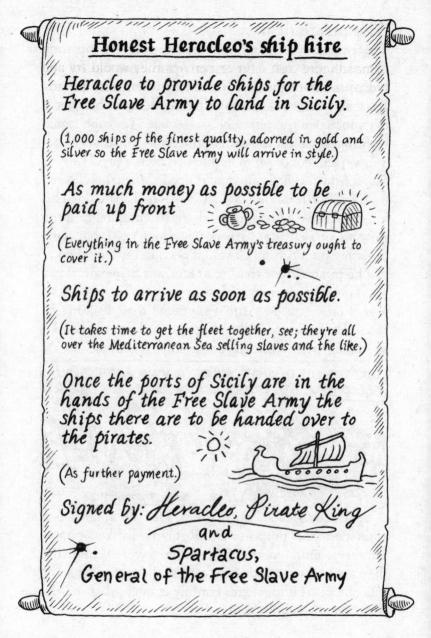

Honest Heracleo's ship hire

Heracleo to provide ships for the Free Slave Army to land in Sicily.

(1,000 ships of the finest quality, adorned in gold and silver so the Free Slave Army will arrive in style.)

As much money as possible to be paid up front

(Everything in the Free Slave Army's treasury ought to cover it.)

Ships to arrive as soon as possible.

(It takes time to get the fleet together, see; they're all over the Mediterranean Sea selling slaves and the like.)

Once the ports of Sicily are in the hands of the Free Slave Army the ships there are to be handed over to the pirates.

(As further payment.)

Signed by: *Heracleo, Pirate King*

and

Spartacus,
General of the Free Slave Army

Of course, Spartacus knew that the pirates were a bit dodgy, they weren't pirates for nothing. They might demand more cash later or perhaps they would try and kidnap some of the slaves and turn them into pirates. But Spartacus was fairly sure that in the end they would deliver.

All he could do was wait and see.

{THE WALL OF DEATH}

While Spartacus was waiting for his ships to come in Crassus hadn't been idle. After the humiliation of Mummius, Crassus was being extra cautious. First he sent a message to the senate requesting that Pompey be called back from Spain and Lucullus back from Asia, where he had been finishing off Mithridates's forces. Asking for help must have really been difficult for a proud man like Crassus. But Crassus knew that injured pride was better than an injured body in battle against Spartacus. He would need all the help he could get.

Crassus marched his army down to just below Thurii. With the whole of the Free Slave Army camped around Rhegium, Crassus didn't want to get too close. (Mummius had ignored that advice and look what had happened to him.) Instead, Crassus wanted to wait for reinforcements before attacking. He wasn't the type of commander to let his army sit around doing nothing and after experiencing Crassus's version of military discipline the Romans probably didn't want to be caught idling around either. It was time to bring out the digging equipment once more.

Crassus was a shrewd commander. He'd noticed that the land south of Thurii was under 35 miles across. So he decided to get his soldiers to dig a trench and build a wall across it. It was a massive job but Crassus was determined to see it through. If he could complete the wall he might be able to simply starve the slaves into submission.

Spartacus could see what Crassus was doing. But the Thracian didn't care. For him the future of the Free Slave Army lay south, across the Strait of Messina. Occasionally, for a bit of fun, the slaves would throw burning sticks into the trench. Sometimes they'd fire arrows at the Romans, but generally they let the Roman soldiers toil away on Crassus's wall. If Spartacus wasn't bothered about the wall, why should the rest of the Free Slave Army worry about it?

Never trust a pirate

As the autumn of 72 BC gradually turned into winter, Crassus's plan began to have an effect. There was no longer any food to be had around Rhegium. With his wall finished, Crassus was able to stop the slaves getting any supplies from the rest of Italy.

As if that wasn't bad enough for Spartacus, it was also becoming clear that the pirates had no intention of returning to help the Free Slave Army…

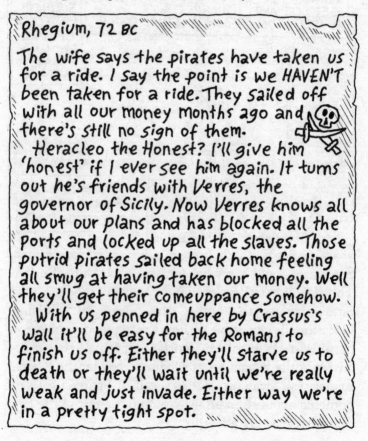

Rhegium, 72 BC

The wife says the pirates have taken us for a ride. I say the point is we HAVEN'T been taken for a ride. They sailed off with all our money months ago and there's still no sign of them.

Heracleo the Honest? I'll give him 'honest' if I ever see him again. It turns out he's friends with Verres, the governor of Sicily. Now Verres knows all about our plans and has blocked all the ports and locked up all the slaves. Those putrid pirates sailed back home feeling all smug at having taken our money. Well they'll get their comeuppance somehow.

With us penned in here by Crassus's wall it'll be easy for the Romans to finish us off. Either they'll starve us to death or they'll wait until we're really weak and just invade. Either way we're in a pretty tight spot.

Everyone in the camp is beginning to realize how bad things are. I dread to think what will happen when it dawns on them there's no ships and no way back north. As usual it's the Gauls that are complaining the loudest. They're starting to demand a separate camp again, and they're questioning my command. Seems some of them think they can do better. After all that hard work getting the Free Slave Army unified again it could all fall apart (again!). If that happens Crassus won't even have to attack us. We'll probably be too busy killing each other.

To make matters worse the winter of 72–71 BC was turning out to be a real stinker. Storms and winds were lashing the exposed slave camp.

Not only that, but news reached Spartacus that Crassus's army would soon be joined by Pompey's forces. If Lucullus also returned to Italy, the Free Slave Army would be left facing a huge number of Roman soldiers. And these weren't just any soldiers – they were the finest military men Rome had to offer.

If the Free Slave Army couldn't cross to Sicily, it was up to Spartacus to find another way out for his followers.

TIME FOR ANOTHER CUNNING PLAN...

Spartacus decided to turn Crassus's vanity against him. He knew that the Roman really wanted to defeat the Free Slave Army all by himself. If Pompey and Lucullus arrived before Crassus had his chance to beat Spartacus, it would be they, and not Crassus, who would take the glory. Crassus would appear to have been too weak to defeat a bunch of slaves without help. The former shepherd from Thrace was about to try his hand at Roman power politics.

Spartacus called together his commanders to explain his plan. Then Spartacus sent a messenger to Crassus with an offer of a peaceful end to the stalemate. Perhaps it ran something like this:

> **Dear Crassus,**
> I'm sure you're as sick of this horrible winter weather as we all are. Perhaps you'd like to meet up and discuss terms for a peaceful settlement of the current crisis? If we can conclude a peace treaty you'll get the credit for 'winning' this worrisome war instead of having to let Pompey and Lucullus 'help' you out.
>   I suggest the following get-out clauses:
>
> I. You 'capture' the remaining gladiators (myself included)
> II. You let the rest of the Free Slave Army 'escape'.

III. You thumb your nose at Pompey and Lucullus and return to Rome victorious.

IV. You take us gladiators back to Rome to parade at your victory celebrations. (We could even fight in the arena for you. Or die on the cross, we're not that worried either way.)

If you'd like to know more about this offer please reply by return messenger. Remember, it's good to talk.

Yours sincerely,

Spartacus the Gladiator General

PS Congratulations on your impressive wall, it really is a big 'un. Of course, it won't stop us breaking out if we're forced to.

In return for the lives of the gladiators, Spartacus was hoping to buy the lives of the rest of his army.

The Roman general must have been sorely tempted. But in the end, the thought of negotiating with a lowly slave offended Crassus too much. The Roman answer was clear:

Dear Spartyscum,
No way. You're all for the cross. Yours, Crassus the Roman General, richest man in all Rome, soon to be Dictator etc. etc. etc.

Once again the Thracian general called together his commanders. It was time to think up a Plan B, and fast.

I. BUILD RAFTS AND USE THEM TO CROSS THE STRAIT.

AREN'T THE SICILIANS EXPECTING US NOW?

WALL

146

Spartacus and his commanders knew that the only real option was to break through Crassus's wall. But before the army did anything Spartacus wanted to make sure they knew what they were up against. So he issued two orders:

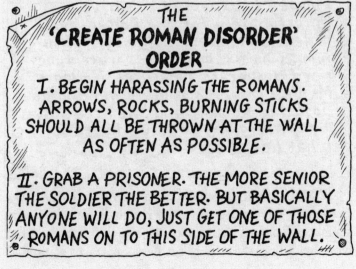

THE
**'CREATE ROMAN DISORDER'
ORDER**

I. BEGIN HARASSING THE ROMANS. ARROWS, ROCKS, BURNING STICKS SHOULD ALL BE THROWN AT THE WALL AS OFTEN AS POSSIBLE.

II. GRAB A PRISONER. THE MORE SENIOR THE SOLDIER THE BETTER. BUT BASICALLY ANYONE WILL DO, JUST GET ONE OF THOSE ROMANS ON TO THIS SIDE OF THE WALL.

Soldiers from the Free Slave Army began to plague the Roman positions. They fired slingshot, spears, arrows and the occasional rock at the wall. Small groups crept across the trench and attacked any Roman foolish enough to be out in the open. One such legionary found himself being dragged, alive, back across the trench and into the slave camp.

Rhegium, 72 BC

Last night I had a word or two with the Roman Prisoner. He didn't want to answer any questions but after we 'persuaded' him to answer he was very helpful. He told us where the wall's weak points are, when the guards change over and when Pompey is expected to arrive. Unfortunately for the Roman, his ordeal isn't over. I'm going to use him as an example. Desperate times need desperate measures. No more Mr Nice Guy. It's time to get tough. Both the Romans and the Free Slave Army are going to have to learn what lies ahead.

Of course, Spartacus had been pretty tough in the past (you don't live in the army, survive gladiator school and slaughter Romans without being a little bit brutal) but what he did next was quite ruthless. Spartacus wanted to remind his soldiers of just why they needed to fight on. He knew there were dark days ahead (and not just because it was winter). To do that he was prepared to be really cruel to the Roman. Just as he'd done when he held funeral games to honour Crixus, Spartacus was using the Roman's cruelty against them to prove a point.

Spartacus selected a patch of ground between the Roman wall and the Free Slave Army camp so both sides could see what was happening. Then he crucified the Roman in full view of everyone...

THIS IS WHAT THEY'LL DO TO US ALL IF THEY EVER CATCH US.

OK, YOU'VE MADE YOUR POINT. CAN I GET DOWN NOW?

For up to three days the poor Roman hung on the cross as a grisly lesson for the Free Slave Army and the Romans. Any Roman expecting the slaves to meekly surrender to them might just as well pack up and go home.

But Spartacus hadn't finished teaching the Romans a lesson. Roman defensive walls were famous throughout the known world as unbreakable. (Just check out Hadrian's Wall in the north of England if you want to see why.) But the ex-gladiator wasn't going to let a mere trench and wall get him down. Once again he waited until the time was right, then put yet another bold plan into action.

The hole-in-the-wall gang

In the middle of winter the Romans celebrated the festival of Saturnalia. Paying homage to the great god Saturn involved a lot of drinking, feasting and general partying. Gambling was allowed in public, executions were cancelled and often military campaigns were postponed. Crassus didn't allow his troops to observe the festivities but they probably found a way to celebrate anyway. After all, who was going to know if a few men had a few drinks and a game of dice to honour Saturn? The slave army was stuck behind the wall and couldn't do anything, could they?

But in the middle of the night (while most of the Romans were no doubt sleeping off their hangovers) Spartacus struck.

FIRST THE FREE SLAVE ARMY FILLED IN A SECTION OF THE TRENCH.

SPARTACUS AND HIS BEST SOLDIERS ATTACKED THE WALL ACROSS THE FILLED TRENCH, MAKING A HOLE IN IT.

CRASH!

UH, OH!

Once again, Spartacus had showed the Romans that he couldn't be penned in. Spartacus and his slave army were free once more.

'I'M SPARTACUS!'

The Free Slave Army lost 12,000 soldiers when they smashed through Crassus's wall, but they weren't all that was lost. Tents, equipment, carts and wagons had all been sacrificed to fill the trench. Without all their equipment the survivors of the Free Slave Army were able to get away quickly, but it would take time to replace all their supplies.

THE SOONER WE GET A NEW WAGON, THE BETTER!

After the breakout came another break-up. Once again it was the Gauls who decided they no longer wanted to follow Spartacus. Gannicus and Castus split away from the main body of the Free Slave Army. Taking around 20,000 soldiers each, they set up camp next to a lake in Lucania. Meanwhile, Spartacus was to take the remaining slaves (around 60,000 of them) and march for the port of Brundisium. There, he planned to seize the town and enough ships to take them back north.

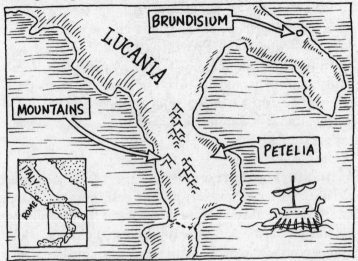

It's possible that the split was caused by ill feeling. Certainly the army was divided again over what to do next. But there is another possible reason. After failing to invade Sicily, Spartacus may have been trying a new tactic: guerrilla warfare.

Er, not quite. With the army split up into smaller units the Romans would have a tougher time tracking them down. It would certainly buy the armies time.

Whatever the reason for the split, Spartacus and his band of followers began their march towards the port city of Brundisium. Spartacus knew that time was running short. Pompey had already arrived in Rome and Lucullus would be arriving somewhere in Italy soon. The trip to Brundisium would be fairly short (only around 100 miles) but they needed to cover the ground quickly.

Crassus's surprise

While Spartacus was setting out east, Gannicus and Castus began discussing the best tactics for the coming campaign. Maybe they were thinking that Crassus would take a few days to pack up his digging equipment. They were wrong.

Crassus knew that Pompey would soon arrive to 'help' him end the slave wars. This was terrible news for the ambitious Roman. When Crassus had asked for Pompey to come back he'd been reeling from Mummius's defeat. Since then, Crassus had become convinced that he could beat Spartacus (and win the glory) by himself. The idea of his bitter rivals getting in on the act drove Crassus crazy. Instead of waiting at the wall, Crassus followed the Free Slave Army almost immediately. His scouts had seen the slave army split and reported that the largest section had moved off, along with Spartacus. Now Crassus believed he had a recipe for victory...

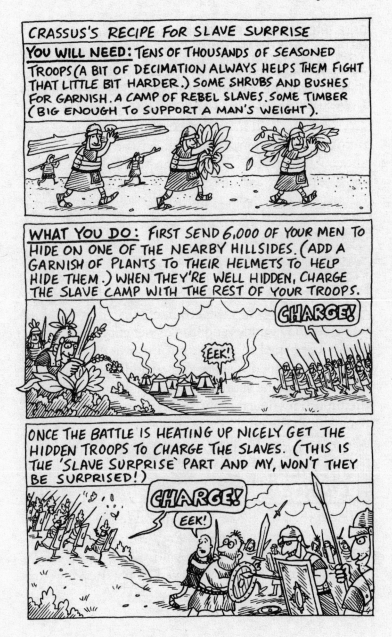

CRASSUS'S RECIPE FOR SLAVE SURPRISE

YOU WILL NEED: TENS OF THOUSANDS OF SEASONED TROOPS (A BIT OF DECIMATION ALWAYS HELPS THEM FIGHT THAT LITTLE BIT HARDER.) SOME SHRUBS AND BUSHES FOR GARNISH. A CAMP OF REBEL SLAVES. SOME TIMBER (BIG ENOUGH TO SUPPORT A MAN'S WEIGHT).

WHAT YOU DO: FIRST SEND 6,000 OF YOUR MEN TO HIDE ON ONE OF THE NEARBY HILLSIDES. (ADD A GARNISH OF PLANTS TO THEIR HELMETS TO HELP HIDE THEM.) WHEN THEY'RE WELL HIDDEN, CHARGE THE SLAVE CAMP WITH THE REST OF YOUR TROOPS.

CHARGE!

EEK!

ONCE THE BATTLE IS HEATING UP NICELY GET THE HIDDEN TROOPS TO CHARGE THE SLAVES. (THIS IS THE 'SLAVE SURPRISE' PART AND MY, WON'T THEY BE SURPRISED!)

CHARGE!

EEK!

ONCE THE SLAVES ARE PROPERLY SLAUGHTERED, CRUCIFY ANY REMAINING ONES. (A SLAVE DEFEAT ISN'T A SLAVE DEFEAT WITHOUT A COUPLE OF CRUCIFIXIONS.) SIT BACK AND SAVOUR THE SWEET, SWEET TASTE OF GORY GLORY. (EVEN BETTER IF YOUR RIVALS BRING ALONG A LARGE SLICE OF HUMBLE PIE TO ACCOMPANY THE VICTORY.)

Sure enough Gannicus and Castus weren't expecting an attack. They tried to retreat, but this was exactly what Crassus had hoped for. For once the Roman had the upper hand and he wasn't about to let the upstart slaves slip through his fingers again. It was time to add his secret ingredient to the mix.

But to Crassus's surprise it wasn't a crack squad of Roman legionaries that charged down from the hill. It was Spartacus and the Free Slave Army.

The slaves united

Two women from Spartacus's army had seen Crassus's soldiers 'hiding' on the hillside.

The women had guessed Crassus's plan and had run to tell Spartacus. Immediately the gladiator general rushed back. He quickly gave the hidden soldiers a good hiding.

Then Spartacus marched back to the camp at the lake. Now facing the whole Free Slave Army, the Romans began to think twice about the last attack. No doubt they were also wondering what had happened to their hidden comrades. None the less, Crassus sent them into battle at the lake again.

The Free Slave Army held their line. Spartacus, their legendary gladiator general, was by their side and they were prepared to die fighting. Still the killing continued. Even after Spartacus arrived Crassus was able to slaughter over 12,000 slaves.

But Crassus's legions were tiring. If the battle continued, the Romans might lose their advantage. So, rather than continue the fight, Crassus allowed his forces to slowly withdraw.

Spartacus also withdrew. Along with what remained of Castus's and Gannicus's forces (which wasn't much) he again set out for Brundisium.

Invite to a fight

After the battle Crassus noticed two things. First, of the 12,300 slaves killed after Spartacus had entered the fight, only two of them had been wounded in the back. Perhaps now even Crassus had to admit that Spartacus inspired a special kind of loyalty from his followers. Over 12,000 slaves had died holding the line with Spartacus rather than turning to run for their lives.

Second, Crassus realized he had a golden opportunity (and Crassus did like his gold) to finish the job on his own. Pompey was still several days away and Spartacus was now nearby. If Crassus could destroy Spartacus and the slaves now he would be the undisputed Roman champion of the slave wars. Crassus tried everything he could think of to provoke Spartacus into another battle.

Dear Spartipants (aka Slave Scum),

We all know you are doomed to die on a cross. After your shameful displays of defiance it's all you can expect. Especially from such civilized people as us Romans. However, I have a suggestion. Rather than letting Pompey and Lucullus in on your defeat why not let me relieve you of your life? It would be such a shame if those two idiots had to be involved, don't you agree?

In return I'll only kill as many of your followers as want to die (and maybe a few more).

Meet me and my forces somewhere in Lucania for a get-together. You know it makes sense.

Yours sincerely,
Marcus Licinius Crassus

PS Fancy telling me how you get your boys to hold the line so well? I use decimation but they don't seem to like it.

Spartacus ignored the Roman's goading. He wasn't interested in fighting another big battle. He had a responsibility to the former slaves who had chosen to follow him. The gladiator wasn't afraid of death himself but he knew Crassus would exact a terrible revenge on his followers. The thought of thousands of crosses planted across the Italian countryside drove him on towards Brundisium.

Fearing that Spartacus would escape his clutches, Crassus sent two of his senior officers after him. Quintus and Scrofa had orders to provoke Spartacus into a battle. At first they failed miserably. Spartacus continued on his way, ignoring the two Romans and their occasional raids on the slave column. But then Spartacus received some very bad news…

~ The Legion ~

LUCIUS LICINIUS LUCULLUS LANDS!

BRUNDISIUM WELCOMES WINNER

One of Rome's finest fighting figures is paying Brundisium a brief visit. General Lucullus has arrived back in Italy after a hard-fought campaign against Mischievous Mithridates. The dashing commander is dashing to the aid of Marcus Licinius Crassus. With Lucky Lucullus on his side Crassus will finally defeat the evil Spartacus and his band of renegade slaves.

Native Bruns turned out in their hundreds to welcome the general. The fortunate few that could hear the masterly military man were treated to a rare speech:

'I'm not here for some parade,' the general told the crowd. 'I'm here to kill that upstart Spartacus. I should have done it years ago. He was one of my soldiers you know. Imagine getting Crassus to do it. He might have a lot of money but he's got no military muscle.'

Scrofa so good

Spartacus immediately halted the march towards the port. He remembered Old 'Triple-L' from his days as a Roman soldier. He would need time to come up with yet another plan, so the Free Slave Army made camp in the Petelia mountains.

But the Romans refused to leave Spartacus in peace. Scrofa and Quintus saw their chance. They attacked the slave camp.

Big mistake.

161

When the Romans rode in for a raid Spartacus unleashed the full force of his reunited army. Suddenly the raiders were being raided and they did not like it. The Free Slave Army, glad to be back in battle, ripped through the Roman lines. Once again the famed Roman discipline broke and the soldiers ran. It was only by chance that Scrofa escaped. Severely wounded by the rampaging slaves, he had to be dragged from the field of battle.

Back at the slave camp the Free Slave Army celebrated as though they'd beaten Crassus himself...

Scrofa and Quintus had succeeded in provoking the slaves (even if they hadn't planned to do it quite that way). The slaves now believed they could take on anyone and win. They argued with Spartacus that they should march straight at Crassus, beat him, then take on Pompey, then Lucullus.

But Spartacus wasn't fooled. He knew that Crassus's army was still intact. The Free Slave Army wasn't gathering newly freed slaves in the way it had in the past. Slave owners were taking far greater care to ensure their slaves didn't run off. Those that wanted to run off, or were brave enough to run off, had already done so. More importantly, the people of Italy, slave and Roman alike, had seen Spartacus walk into Crassus's trap while trying to take Sicily. They'd heard about the slaughter at the lake. In fact the only people that didn't think the Free Slave Army was doomed seemed to be the Free Slave Army itself.

But Spartacus wasn't the type to abandon his friends and back out of a fight. He would stand alongside the slaves who'd risked everything to follow him. What he really needed was a plan…

Petelia mountains, 71 BC

We are surrounded on all sides by bloodthirsty Romans. If we win the next battle all we can expect is another and another and another… For some reason it reminds me of Batiatus's school and the arena.

At least this time the stage is bigger. The whole world is watching. My next plan has to be my best yet.

We could go for Lucullus first. If we beat him at least we'll be through to the port at Brundisium. The problem is no one wants to go north so why bother seizing the port? Life would be so much easier if we all wanted to go home instead of changing the world. The wife says we've already changed the world – a bit. Well, it's not enough as far as I'm concerned...

If we head west we come up against Crassus. To hear the rest of the slave camp talk you'd think Crassus was already beaten. Just because we thumped Scrofa and Quintus doesn't mean Crassus is down and out. But the camp does have a point. He has been weakened. (Besides, beating the richest Roman of them all would be a fine thing to do!)

Let's face it, fighting Crassus is the best option. 1. His army is prone to legging it when we turn up. 2. If we head that way Pompey will be forced to stay in Rome in case we decide to attack the city.

So, Spartacus was going to lead his army back west. Back through Lucania and the burnt-out cities of Nares and Polla.

Back also towards Capua and the still burnt-out school of Batiatus. Back towards Crassus.

Crassus crosses the countryside

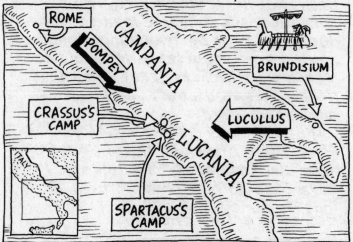

Of course this was exactly what Crassus had hoped the slaves would do. (That's probably why he didn't kill Scrofa and Quintus for being useless.) With Spartacus heading back through Lucania, Crassus would have one last chance to finish him off before Pompey arrived on the scene. At last Crassus's golden opportunity had arrived.

The Free Slave Army got as far as the source of the Silarus river just on the border between Lucania and Campania. There they established their camp once again. Just a few miles away Crassus was doing the same.

The Silarus river, 71 BC

So, this is it. The coming battle will be decisive. With Crassus out of the way Pompey will have to retreat, we'll recruit enough slaves to beat Crassus and then all roads will lead to Rome! If we lose? Well, if we lose all roads will still lead to Rome, we just won't be travelling along them very comfortably. It would be terrible if the Free Slave Army was to be defeated now... after all we've achieved.

The wife says I mustn't worry: 'The Free Slave Army will live on even if you die, Spartacus,' she told me. I mean, would it kill her to be a bit positive once in a while?

> Anyway, it's time to get ready for the coming campaign.
> I hope the rest of the Free Slave Army understands how important this battle is. Perhaps I should think up another show for them, just to make sure...

Once again Spartacus was prepared to be brutal to make a point to his slave army. He told one of the slaves to bring him his horse. This was the same horse Spartacus had stolen from Varinius two years ago. He'd ridden it the length of Italy (twice) and was now going to use it one last time.

IF WE WIN THIS BATTLE I WILL HAVE MY PICK OF THE HORSES THAT BELONG TO THE ENEMY, IF WE LOSE, THEN I WILL HAVE NO NEED OF A HORSE!

HOW'S THAT FOR GRATITUDE?!

With the killing of Spartacus's horse the stage was set for another huge battle. The Free Slave Army knew that their leader would stay with them to the very last.

Spartacus vs Crassus: The showdown

Spartacus had hardly finished killing his horse when some of his troops broke ranks. They attacked the Roman's defences and began fighting Crassus's soldiers.

The battle had begun. With Spartacus at their head the rest of the Free Slave Army charged the Roman lines. But this time the Roman soldiers (probably scared of another decimation) held their line.

Again and again the slaves charged the Roman lines, but they could not break through them. Spartacus himself tried to break through and engage Crassus directly, but the Roman soldiers had learnt their lesson. This time the Free Slave Army were not victorious.

169

Spartacus fought so bravely and the battle was so epic that even Roman writers had to give his performance rave reviews. Let's leave it to them to describe his final moments in the battle:

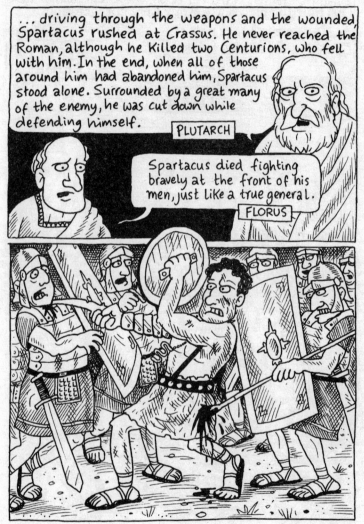

Spartacus took a spear wound to his thigh. Collapsing on one knee, he held his shield up in front of him and fought off those who were attacking him, until he and the large number of men around him were finally surrounded and cut down. The killing was on such a scale that it was not possible to count the dead. The body of Spartacus was never found.

APPIAN

The Free Slave Army was no more. The news that their leader, the gladiator hero, was dead was too much for the remaining slaves. Tired out and weakened after losing tens of thousands of soldiers, they were defeated.

More than 60,000 slaves were slaughtered. The slave survivors eventually fled the battlefield. Unfortunately for them (and for Crassus) they ran straight into Pompey's legions. Pompey's men killed many of them but took around 6,000 prisoners. Of course, Pompey wasted no time telling Rome it was he who'd finally crushed the slave uprising.

THAT POMPOUS POMPEY!

The 6,000 prisoners were all that remained of an army that had once numbered well over 100,000. Of course, Crassus wasn't about to let those prisoners live. Especially since no one seemed able to confirm that Spartacus was definitely dead. Perhaps the Thracian gladiator was one of the 6,000.

Crassus and Pompey weren't taking any chances…

From Capua, the scene of the original gladiator breakout two years before, to Rome, 6,000 wooden crosses were set up. On each one a free slave died…

Epilogue

Prisoners weren't the only things the Romans recovered from the defeated Free Slave Army. They also found dozens of other trophies, each one showing how successfully Spartacus had led his army for two years:

TROPHIES RECOVERED:

5 ROMAN EAGLES
(AS CARRIED BY THE ROMAN LEGIONS DEFEATED BY SPARTACUS)

5 FASCES
(AS CARRIED, AND DROPPED, BY VARIOUS ROMAN COMMANDERS)

26 BATTLE STANDARDS
(AS CARRIED BY THE ROMAN BATTALIONS DEFEATED BY SPARTACUS)
ALSO:

3,000 ROMAN CITIZENS

For years after the slave uprising the Romans remained terrified of Spartacus. Every time a slave murdered his master the Romans remembered him. They worried that Spartacus was still alive and would come back to raise his Free Slave Army again. Small bands of escaped slaves and poor peasants occasionally appeared in southern Italy. But the Romans didn't take any chances. These small groups were mercilessly crushed. Rome could not afford another Spartacus.

If you're wondering what happened to Crassus and Pompey, they eventually got what was coming to them. After defeating Spartacus they both became famous politicians and military men (despite the fact they despised one another). Crassus was killed in 53 BC leading yet another invasion. His head was cut off and used as a prop in a play, much to the amusement of his enemies. Pompey the Great went on to crush the pirates (serves them right!) before falling out with Julius Caesar. He was murdered in Egypt in 48 BC.

Of course, there are long histories written about each of the Roman generals and what they did next. After all, these were famous, rich Romans, leaders of the 'civilized' world.

As for Spartacus, the fact that there was anything written about the Thracian shepherd boy at all shows just how inspirational he was. He took on the Romans and came very close to beating them. He showed them that a slave could more than hold his own against them. We don't know for certain that he died in that final battle, but his legend lived on to give hope to the people who suffered under the Roman Empire. Those who followed him were prepared to sacrifice their lives for their freedom. Freedom which Spartacus tried to make real.

It is no surprise that the story of Spartacus has become famous through books, films, ballets and even football (who do you think Spartak Moscow are named after?). His name has inspired people throughout history. Two thousand years after his death famous revolutionaries like Karl Marx and the German 'Spartacists' used his name to inspire their own struggle. Whenever people are mistreated, exploited and generally downtrodden they can identify with the Thracian shepherd boy whose boyhood dream of becoming a hero took him into the history books.